# WHY SHOULD GUYS HAVE ALL THE FUN?

# LOIDA LEWIS

AND

## BLAIR S. WALKER

# WHY SHOULD GUYS HAVE ALL THE FUN?

AN Asian American Story
of Love, Marriage,
Motherhood, and Running
a Billion-Dollar Empire

## WILEY

Published by John Wiley & Sons, Inc., Hoboken, New Jersey.
Published simultaneously in Canada.

For general information on our other products and services or for technical support, please contact our Customer Care Department within the United States at (800) 762-2974, outside the United States at (317) 572-3993 or fax (317) 572-4002.

Wiley also publishes its books in a variety of electronic formats. Some content that appears in print may not be available in electronic formats. For more information about Wiley products, visit our web site at www.wiley.com.

*Library of Congress Cataloging-in-Publication Data is Available:*

ISBN 9781119989837 (Cloth)
ISBN 9781119989844 (ePub)
ISBN 9781119989851 (ePDF)

**COVER DESIGN:** PAUL MCCARTHY
**COVER ART:** (PORTRAIT) © **E. LEE WHITE PHOTOGRAPHY**
(FLOWER) © **SHUTTERSTOCK | BONCHAN**

SKY10042389_020223

# DEDICATION

*Ad majorem Dei gloriam*
(To the greater glory of God) – St. Ignatius Loyola

*TO*
*Leslie Malaika Lewis*
*Christian Roy Vincent Hamadun Harelimana Lewis Sword*
*Savilla Joy Innocente Niyonkuru Lewis Sword*

*Gavin Rodney Sword*
*January 26, 1973–April 27, 2022*
*Co-parent with Leslie*
*Father of Christian and Savilla*

*TO*
*Christina Savilla Nicolas Lewis and Daniel Noah Halpern*
*Calvin Reginald Lewis Halpern*
*Sasha Lewis Nicolas Halpern*
*Macy Savilla Lewis Halpern*

# CONTENTS

# PROLOGUE

"All things work together unto good to those who love God, to those who are called according to His purpose."

—Romans 8:28

"Lord, please destroy the cancer that's sapping the life of my beloved soulmate. Father God, have mercy in the name of Your Son, our Lord Jesus Christ. Amen."

Slowly lifting my head from my clasped hands, I make the sign of the cross and then open my eyes onto the sumptuous interior of 834 Fifth Avenue, a breathtaking, 15-room, two-level East Side co-op apartment across the street from Central Park. New Year's Day 1993 was celebrated a few days ago, meaning my family and I have lived in 834 Fifth Avenue less than a month.

My husband, Reginald Lewis, purchased and oversaw the decoration of this exquisite $12-million abode, which holds four upstairs bedrooms, a dining area capable of seating 24, antiques that include two eighteenth-century French writing desks, and masterpieces from artists such as Romare Bearden and Picasso.

I'd sell it all in a heartbeat, if that would obliterate the inoperable brain cancer my spouse is bravely battling.

Ditto Reginald's private jet and our majestic, multimillion-dollar rental home in Paris, where Reginald guides the fortunes of an international food corporation he acquired five years ago for $1 billion.

Wealth has never been my be-all and end-all. At the moment, my top priority is saving the love of my life, the father of our daughters, Leslie and Christina.

If God gave me a choice in the matter, I'd gladly exchange my life for Reginald's. He's the rock our family is anchored to.

My thoughts are interrupted by the voice of our butler, Lucien Stoutt: "Mrs. Lewis, the Reverend Angelo Lando is downstairs."

"Bring him upstairs, Lucien."

Easily the best-known faith healer in the Philippines, my homeland, Lando (not his real name) gives me a firm handshake after striding confidently into the master bedroom. A slightly built man who's pushing 60, he has jet-black hair and looks to be about 5-foot-6. Lando's accompanied by another Filipino who's carrying a black leather bag. I'm guessing it contains what Lando needs to perform psychic surgery on my husband.

As Lando approaches a massage table that's been draped with towels for my spouse's procedure, I draw in a super deep breath and hold it for a second, then exhale slowly.

This desperate faith-healer gambit is my idea, not my husband's.

Few individuals are as analytical, fact-based and no-nonsense as Reginald, who turned 50 last month. When he decided against chemotherapy and radiation treatments in order to protect his diminishing brain function, I secretly wept because I would have opted for both of those regimens.

But once it was clear that Western medicine's top cancer-fighting weapons were off the table, I began looking into the Philippines' rich history of nontraditional medical treatments.

Faith healers do booming business back home. And the best of the best has flown to Manhattan from the Philippines for the express purpose of saving my darling husband.

Reginald initially wanted nothing to do with "that bullshit quackery" as he characterized it, but now that his weakened left side has left him barely able to walk, he's reluctantly agreed. Explaining why Reginald is lying face-up on the massage table, wearing shorts that a towel has been draped over.

Joining me, Reginald, Lando, and Lando's assistant in the huge master bedroom is my brother-in-law, Tony Fugett, who's traveled from Baltimore to assist his stricken sibling. Someone who's been a who's been a godsend since his brother has taken ill, Tony is looking at Lando with unabashed skepticism that borders on hostility.

Clad in a white Cuban shirt and dark slacks, Lando isn't wearing a mask or gloves but has a thick gold ring on his left hand and a hefty gold bracelet on his right wrist.

Picking the black leather bag from the floor, he suddenly thrusts it toward the ceiling and calls out in a booming voice:

> *"Mga espiritu! Alisin ang lahat ng negatibong energies mula sa katawan ni Reg Lewis."*

Not understanding Tagalog, the native language of the Philippines, my husband and Tony are clearly baffled.

I'll tell them later what Lando has just bellowed: "Spirits! Remove all negative energies from Reg Lewis' body."

Now Lando begins silently kneading Reginald's stomach, before making a quick north-to-south incision using only his hands. Torrents of bright red blood begin flowing down Reginald's sides, staining the white towels protecting the massage table.

Alarmed, I peer at my husband's face to see if he's in excruciating pain, but miraculously he seems to be doing just fine. Lando runs his hands and fingers through the massive incision he's created, then starts pulling bloody entrails out of Reginald's midsection . . . even though my husband's cancer is attacking his brain . . . I really want to believe this, I really, really do.

But it doesn't take long to see Lando is relying on impressive sleight of hand and is substituting animal entrails for the cancerous material he's supposedly extracting from my soulmate. As Lando continues his routine, it's clear to Reginald, Tony, and me that the renowned faith healer is merely an opportunistic charlatan, but we allow him to finish his "operation."

When it's over about 15 minutes later, Reginald calmly and courteously thanks Lando, who I direct Lucien to escort downstairs.

Lucien, Lando, and Lando's assistant are barely out the bedroom door before Tony, who has a temper like his older brother, pops off. Noting that Lando was "palming" Reginald and little else, Tony is dead set against Lando receiving his $20,000 fee.

Reginald, who's now sitting upright on the massage table as I numbly wipe fake blood off his stomach and chest, is equally adamant that Lando is getting paid.

"Why am I paying him?" Reginald asks quietly. "Because there was a promise of hope. Is this amount of money worth the promise of hope?

"Yes!"

Hope. I'm armed with something considerably stronger than that, namely, the unparalleled might of my Lord and Savior. I'm able to see Angelo Lando's visit this morning for exactly what it is: a test of my faith.

Nothing I just saw weakened my allegiance in the slightest, which is what God wanted to learn before He blesses my spouse and I with a miracle.

"Darling, we're going to beat this," I tell Reginald as I look him in the eye. Upon hearing this he wraps both arms around me, and I can practically feel the determination emanating from his fierce heart.

With God in our corner, there's no way the malady sabotaging my husband's brain can win.

Map showing CHINA, INDIA, Taiwan, Vietnam, PHILIPPINES, Brunei, Malaysia, Singapore, Indonesia, and SORSOGON. Labeled SOUTHEAST ASIA. Map by Aznefic Agurio

# 1

# THE GIRL FROM SORSOGON

Like most ultra-successful entrepreneurs, my father, Francisco J. Nicolas, Sr., has a knack for peering into the future.

When my mother, Magdalena Mañalac Nicolas, was lugging me around in her belly, Papa sensed that my brothers, Danilo and Jose, would soon have a little sister. Whenever a hunch takes root in my father's hyperactive brain, he leaves nothing to chance when it comes to turning that hunch into reality.

That explains why Papa scours the Philippines in search of a picture of brunette Hollywood actress Deanna Durbin. A huge star during the 1940s, Durbin clearly has something that resonates with my dad, because after locating her photograph, he brings it to our house in the town of Sorsogon and hangs it in my parents' bedroom, right in my expecting mom's line of sight.

He believes that if Mama gazes upon Durbin's image day in and day out, I'll *have* to come out a girl! Perhaps one resembling Durbin, a cute, young White woman with an ample forehead, high cheekbones, and winsome smile?

If this sounds off-the-wall, eccentricities and willful ways are part of Papa's charm. Weeks before Mama's due date, Papa strolls onto a Sorsogon field where several water buffalo he owns are kept. After carefully inspecting the beasts, my father hand-picks one to fulfill the sacred duty of pulling a cart that will transport him and Mama to the hospital for my birth.

You can't let a water buffalo full of negative energy pull your wife and newborn child around town, right?

When my mother's contractions begin the morning of December 23, 1942, the designated water buffalo is hitched to our cart, and my parents set off for Sorsogon Provincial Hospital. With World War II under way and the Philippines besieged by Japanese occupiers, most Filipinos aren't driving cars, in part because Japanese soldiers have no qualms about commandeering every operational civilian vehicle they encounter.

So, my solidly upper-middle-class parents ride in an animal-drawn cart to the medical facility where Dr. Saturnino Lopez helps me draw my first breath. Despite being born into noteworthy affluence, my first ride is in a creaky wooden cart that trails a smelly water buffalo! War and pestilence are great equalizers indeed.

As we head home from the hospital, my parents and I roll past smiling, waving fishermen and farmers, the primary residents of Sorsogon Province. Papa, who's built a lucrative lumber and furniture business in Sorsogon Province, is universally admired thanks to his kindness and generosity.

Mama, on the other hand, elicits province-wide fear and trepidation, thanks to her terrifically exacting nature. Like Papa, Mama also thought I was going to be a girl, which is why she put up with Deanna Durbin's cheerful, intrusive gaze while waiting to deliver me.

I spend the bulk of my childhood in a huge two-story concrete house that's the most prominent dwelling in the town of Sorsogon, as well as the only one with a drugstore, bowling alley, gasoline station, billiard tables, a lumber business on the first floor, and living quarters on the second.

As children are prone to do, I spend a lot of time quietly observing the interpersonal dynamic between my parents. There's no question Mama is every bit as strong-willed and set in her ways as Papa. That sets the stage for a lot of bickering, which is usually due to their differing management approaches when dealing with the many workers our family employs.

One particularly spirited quarrel kicks off after a carpenter arrives at our house to tackle a project but fails to bring the tools he needs to do the job properly. When Mama discovers this, she immediately begins pummeling the poor man with blistering sarcasm.

When my father hears the commotion and has the audacity to object on the carpenter's behalf, this sparks a disagreement that's considerably louder and more fiercely contested than the usual knock-down, drag-out shouting matches Papa and Mama are always having.

Papa always sides with the poor, the oppressed, society's have-nots. I embrace this same worldview, as do my brothers and my sister, Imelda, who was born a few years after me. But like Mama, I have a hard time dealing with people who are incompetent, inefficient, and lacking in focus and common sense. I just happen to be more tactful than Mama when encountering someone's inadequacies but, like her, I can also be stern and uncompromising.

Lest I leave the impression that my early days are dominated by strife and turmoil, my childhood is actually very joyful. My parents may have markedly different personalities, but they deeply love each other and always sing from the same sheet music when it comes to loving and nurturing their children.

## THE PAST IS PROLOGUE

During those times when my parents aren't around, it falls on my older brothers Danilo and Jose to show me how the world works. Their lessons tend to be more entertaining than Papa's and Mama's, so I'm over the moon when an opportunity arises to hang out with my brothers and some of their buddies in a Manila neighborhood where Mama's parents own a big home.

An energetic and inquisitive 5-year-old attempting to stave off boredom on a blisteringly hot summer day, I'm about to discover that the Almighty has ordered one of His most vigilant guardian angels to watch over me. As I play with Danilo, 10, Jose, 7, and their pals alongside an empty dirt road, far in the distance a tiny plume of tan dust materializes and silently grows larger as it creeps toward us. We all watch this development with eager grins.

Traffic has been sporadic in the Philippines since World War II ended two years earlier, thanks to the fact that a large number of roads and bridges are pockmarked with massive bomb craters. The national economy is pretty bombed out, too, leaving Filipinos without much disposable income for purchasing and maintaining cars, trucks, and scooters.

Consequently, the sight of a vehicle coming our way has my brothers and their friends chattering excitedly. How better to spice up an unremarkable Philippine day than with a Kamikaze dash in front of an oncoming car!

"*Takot ka ba, Loida?*" (Are you scared, Loida?) my brothers and their friends taunt in singsong Tagalog, our native tongue. "*Takot ka ba?*"

No, not in the least. Not many things generate fear inside prepubescent brains, including scenarios that could easily result in grievous bodily harm or death. Likely assuming that I'm too petrified with fear to join them, my brothers and their buddies flit across the dirt road well in advance of the fast-moving vehicle, which is almost upon us now and resembles a landlocked olive-green battleship trailing a brownish wake.

A U.S. Army truck.

"*Takot ka ba?*" Here's your answer, fellas!

Intent on pulling off a daring sprint that will be the stuff of legend and that will make these silly boys stop equating frilly cotton dresses with timidity, I start running as fast as my little legs can propel me. About four paces into my mad dash, the world unexpectedly goes topsy-turvy. The blue of the sky and brown of the dirt road begin to intermingle in rapid-fire fashion, punctuated by a terrifying CRUNCH! When the herky-jerky kaleidoscope finally stops turning, I find myself sprawled awkwardly on the ground, listening to blood-curdling screams from my brothers as a roiling cloud of thick brown dust nearly obscures the sun.

I also hear soul-rending wailing that could be coming from only one person—my mother. How did she get here?

Mercifully, a little greenish-blue apron that was draped over my dress got entangled in one of the truck's huge wheels, resulting in my right foot getting crushed, but saving me from being completely smashed beneath a gargantuan tire like a cyan-colored bug.

Perhaps due to the onset of shock, I don't feel any pain as I listen to the truck's diesel engine clatter to a stop, followed by the sound of several deep, anxious-sounding voices. In no time, Mama is hovering over and comforting me, and she's quickly joined by a group of dark-complexioned men who have close-cropped black hair and are clad in green military uniforms. From my vantage point on the ground, they all look to be at least 10 feet tall.

They're babbling excitedly in an incomprehensible language, but it's clear from their tone of voice that they're nearly as frightened as I am. One of the soldiers quietly squats beside Mama, before picking me up with a combination of tenderness and strength I've only felt at the hands of my father.

I must have passed out at that point, because the next thing I remember is being in a hospital bed inside a U.S. Army medical facility, feeling an eerie numbness on my right foot.

After getting discharged, I spend several months hobbling around in a white plaster cast that encases my foot and ankle, a small price to pay in light of what could have unfolded. My injury transforms me into a neighborhood celebrity whose friends and family sweetly scribble touching messages on my cast.

A post-crash activity I've come to enjoy is watching my parents put the fear of God into my brothers Danilo and Jose, who are admonished repeatedly for not taking better care of their little sister. While I do get a kick out of this, I feel sad whenever I think back to the mournful sounds that came from my Mama and brothers while I laid crumpled in the dirt. I don't ever want to be a source of pain or discomfort for my family again.

There's a saying that goes "the past is prologue," which definitely proves to be true where my mishap is concerned.

First, getting mowed down by a huge military truck and escaping largely unscathed is confirmation that God holds me firmly in His loving, protective embrace. Moving forward, I never doubt that the Almighty is my strength and my shield, just as Psalm 28 states.

Second, that fateful day won't be the last time an African American man sends me flying head over heels and then helps restore my equilibrium with quiet inner strength and compassion.

Third, I learn it's a dumb idea to rubberstamp a plan simply because males have signed off on it. Because even my young mind instantly understood that running in front of that truck might not be the brightest thing to do. Using my accident as a yardstick, in the future I give my feminine intuition much greater weight when mapping out potential courses of action.

## HIGH EXPECTATIONS FROM PAPA

The man who views himself as the king of foreshadowing, Papa, naturally has his own unique take on my accident. To him, my escape from death is simply God's affirmation that I'm going to be a great lawyer, in keeping with Papa's dreams for me. My father attended the University of the Philippines College of Law for two years, but was making so much money from his burgeoning lumber business that he left law school before graduating.

According to my father, I'm tailormade for a legal career, thanks to being articulate, fast-thinking, and someone who gets along with the impoverished and the wealthy equally well. It never occurs to me that Papa might still be a wannabe attorney, even though the Nicfur Furniture business he started in 1940 has prospered impressively.

Papa's keen interest in my future highlights one of the main parenting differences between him and Mama. A pharmacy school graduate, she's a doting mother who's one of my main confidants. Unlike Papa, Mama seems more inclined to allow for free will when it comes to the professions her offspring pursue.

With my father, I get a sense that everything he says and does around me is with an eye toward preparing me for a future he's carefully mapped out. Think Richard Williams and his painstaking programming of tennis superstars Venus and Serena. Papa has a similar, big-picture approach to childrearing.

But here's the thing—as a child, I don't view Papa's nurturing and high expectations as something that's unpleasant or wearisome. I welcome it, especially when you consider that I'm not able to see him most of the week. Monday through Friday he's in Manila running his furniture-manufacturing business, so my siblings and I cherish the weekend time we get to spend with him, following a commute that calls on Papa to fly an hour by plane from Manila to Legaspi, followed by a two-hour car ride to Sorsogon.

The Nicolas kids continually joke about our father's "brainwashing." He's sized up the world, gotten a feel for his children's strengths and weaknesses, and has given us loving shoves toward the path he feels we're best suited for. And I don't think it's a coincidence he always singles out vocations that would prove useful to an entrepreneur like himself!

Regarding his desire for me to be an attorney—what top business-man wouldn't want a daughter who can offer topnotch legal expertise to his enterprise? Papa says my brother Danilo should major in commerce in college, so he can eventually take the helm of my father's companies. Jose is encouraged to focus on civil engineering, which would make him an ideal candidate to take over Papa's construction company at some point.

Papa never pushes Imelda, otherwise known as Mely, toward a particular career field. In my father's estimation, my beautiful sister's looks will enable her to eventually marry a banker. . .a development that could unquestionably benefit Papa down the road.

Meanwhile, he decrees that Francisco, Jr., the baby of the family who's known to all as Francis, would make a wonderful architect. Might that be so Francis can help out with Papa's construction and furniture-manufacturing firms?

## BUSINESS LESSONS AT THE DINNER TABLE

Being raised by Francisco J. Nicolas, Sr., is akin to growing up in a finishing school for entrepreneurs. A lot of his lessons take place on the spacious, second-floor balcony of our house. The entire family is usually present, enjoying a panoramic view of the town of Sorsogon as we devour a sumptuous Saturday dinner Papa has shown our cook how to prepare.

After we finish the main course and one of our maids clears the dishes, we move to the balcony. The family starts munching on apples and grapes as Papa beckons his offspring to form a semicircle around him. What better place to quiz us about running a business and creating affluence?

"Tell me," Papa asks gravely as our smiling mother looks on. "What are the five secrets of success?" Without waiting for an answer, he begins ticking them off. My siblings and I know this stuff backward and forward but wouldn't dream of stealing Papa's thunder.

Number 1 is hard work! Papa was only 11 when he lost his father and was then sent to live with a rich uncle who owned and operated several businesses. My father never misses an opportunity to let us know that he worked his tail off to transform himself into an entrepreneur on par with his kinfolk.

Number 2 is common sense/resourcefulness. Papa spits out anecdotes that showcase his common sense and resourcefulness in business scenarios.

Number 3 is determination, or tenacity, which always prompts Papa to remind us: "If at first you don't succeed, try, try again." Then he segues into examples of how his determination to avoid failure enabled him to overcome seemingly insurmountable obstacles.

Number 4 is thrift, my father's term for managing money so that it makes even more money. Papa may be a generous soul, but at the same time he spends his hard-earned cash prudently. If anyone doubts this, all they have to do is peer over the balcony and look down the side street where my dad's car is parked. He could easily buy a new one but refuses to do so when there are plenty of cheaper, well-maintained used cars available.

Number 5 is faith in God, never a problem in our household, given that we live next to a Catholic church where the parish priest, Mons Florencio Yllana, is Papa's best friend.

I've easily listened to the five secrets of success thousands of times and can recite each verbatim, along with the anecdotes Papa relies on to buttress whatever case he's making. I never tire of his wealth-building advice, though, because I know he wants his kids to live successful lives.

## AT EASE WITH AFFLUENCE

Papa has other aspirations for me, aside from becoming a lawyer. That is why when I turn seven, he builds a movie house in Sorsogon that he christens the Loida Theater. My father confides to Mama that he can see me eventually running for public office after I become an attorney, so having a movie theater with my name on it will build name recognition that will prove useful later!

Thanks to my parents, particularly Papa, self-esteem is never in short supply during my childhood. Combine that with the fact that I love to learn, and the groundwork has been laid for epic academic achievement. Consequently, I'm the salutatorian in my class at Burabud Elementary School, a public school in the town of Sorsogon.

But in time I'm surprised to discover that Mely, who's two grades behind me and also attends Burabud Elementary School, is every bit my equal academically. After Mama observes how her girls routinely obliterate the competition at Burabud Elementary, she concludes we're not being properly challenged.

So, after I move up to sixth grade and Mely graduates to the fourth grade, Mama enrolls us in St. Agnes Academy, a private, all-girls Catholic School in Legaspi City, which is a two-hour car ride from the town of Sorsogon. Mama doesn't seek her kids' opinions about this dramatic move, she simply executes it.

My mother attended St. Agnes Academy when she was in elementary school, had her First Communion at St. Agnes, and wants to expose my sister and me to the school's academic rigor, as well as the Benedictine sisters' spiritual influence. Their mantra, "Ora et Labora" (Pray and work) is deeply ingrained in my and Mely's brains.

At St. Agnes Academy, we find ourselves in a daunting new environment, living in a huge dormitory with 75 other girls enrolled in grades 1 through 12. I become lifelong friends with many of my classmates.

Instead of going home every day, now we return to the town of Sorsogon only once a month. My no-nonsense take on obedience and morality is on display during one of those brief Sorsogon visits. All of 12 years old, I've learned that a businessman in my hometown has gotten a green light to open a topless bar in the central part of town. This makes my youthful skin crawl because I envision the business overrunning my sleepy hometown with prostitutes and their disgusting customers.

I encourage about 15 of my friends to sign a petition to keep a depraved sin den from appearing in the middle of town! Not content to leave things there, I also lead a silent protest in front of the municipal council members who approved the topless bar. My lobbying is successful, and the plan for the topless bar winds up getting canceled.

None of my family members seem surprised to see me, as a pre-teen, organizing a protest worthy of an adult. In fact, my father grinningly informs me afterward that I'm demonstrating why he sees me becoming a lawyer and a politician.

I may be flourishing at St. Agnes, but my younger sister routinely sneaks into my dorm bed at night due to homesickness. When Mama gets wind of this, she pulls Mely out of the school and moves her into a highly rated Sorsogon pilot school, leaving me at St. Agnes by myself.

How do I deal with this potentially destabilizing development? By burrowing under the covers of my dormitory bed and using a flashlight to study after the dorm lights are extinguished. I'm not going to allow Mely's departure to keep me from getting the grades I need to be No. 1 in my class!

While many people might call me demure, I cherish competition, including going head-to-head with some of the Bicol Region's brainiest girls! I wind up the salutatorian of my sixth-grade class and valedictorian when I get my high school diploma from St. Agnes.

Along with acing my studies, during my stay at St. Agnes I dutifully digest two incredibly powerful books that Papa asked me to tackle:

*The Power of Positive Thinking* by Norman Vincent Peale and *How to Win Friends and Influence People* by Dale Carnegie.

How I manage to find time for extracurricular reading, classes, cheerleading, piano lessons, acting in school plays and being elected St. Agnes' student council president is beyond me. No one ever thinks of overachievers as needing to slow down, but by the time I get out of St. Agnes, I'm feeling pretty burned out.

I need a break . . . and can't think of a better time to take one than during my first semester as a college student!

# 2

# "HERE COME THE NICOLASES!"

I've decided to become a nun. I know Papa won't be happy to hear of this because it will upend his plans for me to become a lawyer!

From the days when he used to sit me on his knee, it's been understood that law and politics are to be my calling. That is, until I went off to college and messed things up. Well, it can't be helped because, after all, it's my life. It's hardly as though I'm looking to pursue a vocation that will besmirch the family name.

Plus, shouldn't it count for something if I make myself happy, while simultaneously following what I believe is God's path for me?

I haven't actually entered a nunnery yet, so I've still got time to figure out how to spin things in a way that makes everyone feel good about my decision. Until then, I'm not sharing my nunnery aspiration with anyone.

Not my siblings, not my friends, and especially not Papa.

## CHOOSING A PATH

Thanks to my sterling high school grades, I wind up with a plethora of attractive college options. St. Theresa's College, which is in Manila, gets the nod over another school in the same city, Scholastica's College.

St. Theresa's wins partially because it's closer to Papa's Nicfur Furniture store, which has a small apartment behind the showroom. The apartment will be my home during my stint at St. Theresa's College.

After mistakenly assuming I could stop studying nonstop like I did in high school, and still get top grades. I discover the error of my ways when my first-semester report card arrives. Although I earn 90s in philosophy, literature, history, and mathematics, I receive a 77 in Spanish. Huh? This grade enrages me because it erases any chance I have of being classified magna cum laude or summa cum laude upon graduation.

For three doggone centuries, my country was considered a Spanish colony, until the United States took over the colonizer role around 1898, aborting the Philippines' nascent revolution against Spain.

Spanish was widely spoken throughout the Philippines up till World War II. In fact, Mama's father—Don Roman Mañalac—speaks only in Spanish, as does Mama. So my ear is definitely attuned to the language, yet it still manages to trip me up. Spanish classes are mandatory at all Philippine colleges and universities. Good grief! My ire isn't directed at my instructor but at myself for failing to resort to my usual study habits.

After my less than impressive grade in Spanish, I return to my tried-and-true study routine with single-minded intensity. Plus, I join the Sodality, an organization that honors the Blessed Virgin Mary. And on Fridays, I work with a group that delivers food and clothing to Manila's impoverished and homeless residents.

As if this weren't enough, I also write for the school newsletter, "The Theresian"; lend my talents to a literary publication known as "The ORION"; sign up for a poetry reading group whose members include male students from Ateneo de Manila University; and join a group called "Girls' Friday" that's composed of college women involved with Student Catholic Action.

Despite that strenuous academic/extracurricular load, when commencement day arrives, I receive a liberal arts degree in humanities with cum laude honors. I also get a Catholic Action Award during commencement, to my great surprise!

After graduation, my friend and classmate Violeta Calvo heads off to the University of the Philippines College of Law in Quezon City, while I remain in Manila, where I teach catechism classes in the public school system and work as a Philippines history instructor at Philippines Women's University, a well-known, non-sectarian school. In my characteristic fashion, I also sign up for evening classes offered by the University of the Philippines College of Law in Manila, in lieu of the day law classes offered on the Diliman campus.

After balancing this murderous schedule on the way to earning a year's worth of law school credits, I wise up, decide to attend law school full time, and join Violeta at UP-Diliman, while remaining steadfast in my decision to join a nunnery. Having learned the hard way that legal study requires my undivided attention, I make it a point not to tackle any teaching jobs.

UP-Diliman is a bastion of liberalism, serious scholarship, and is the top educational institution in the country when I enroll in 1963. Many leaders from the worlds of medicine, politics, industry, architecture, and fine arts are UP-Diliman graduates, as are a slew of noteworthy writers.

None of the Catholic-aligned educational institutions in the Philippines are particularly fond of the University of the Philippines, which they consider a hotbed of communism, along with being antagonistic toward Catholicism.

The Catholic academicians hostile to the University of the Philippines would be very surprised to know that one of its students— me—is stealthily attending off-campus, informational sessions where the Notre Dame de Vie Institute talks about nuns and the work that nuns do. I find the Institute attractive because, the nuns associated with it wear ordinary clothes while working as secretaries, teachers, social workers, etc.

The thought of gliding through Quezon City as an incognito nun appeals to me. It would be interesting to rub shoulders with people who are none the wiser that I've taken vows of poverty, obedience, and chastity.

Established by a French priest, the Notre Dame de Vie Institute is a Catholic religious organization with offices located in a small house in Quezon City. I'm one of about 10 young Filipinas from all walks of life who are curious to see what devoting the rest of our lives to God might be like.

As would-be nuns, we all share the same overarching goal: to follow Christ in His spirit of love and service.

After a year of listening to Notre Dame de Vie Institute lectures primarily given by Mother Superior Marie Goux, she challenges me to make the toughest decision of my young life. Noting how seamlessly I've adapted to the Notre Dame de Vie Institute and its mission, Mother Superior tells me that if I intend to take my vows to become a nun, I'll need to start my formal training on July 4, 1965.

Even though I'm currently a second-year student at the University of the Philippines College of Law, I sure could use some wise counsel right now. Mama has always been an invaluable touchstone during times like this, so I need to swallow my pride and unveil the big secret I've been keeping from her.

"Loida," she tells me in a neutral-sounding voice, "you're in your second year of law school, and you have two years left. Wouldn't it make sense to get your law degree and then pass the bar before you enter a nunnery?

"After that, you can go wherever you want to go. Whether you're in a convent or not, that degree will always be yours, and you won't have to depend on anybody."

As always, Mama's thoughtful advice makes a world of sense. The next time I visit the Notre Dame de Vie Institute, it's with the intention of informing Mother Superior that I won't be moving forward with my training come July 4.

"You are like fruit that is not ripe yet," Mother Superior says in that kindly way of hers. "But you are full of integrity, and your motives are pure. And who knows, the fruit may yet fall from the tree."

Mother Superior's response enables me to walk away from the Notre Dame de Vie Institute, and the possibility of becoming a nun, with an untroubled heart. When you are not ready, you are not ready.

Just because becoming a nun is no longer in my future, that doesn't mean I can no longer be of service to people. With that in mind, when my third year of law school rolls around, I seek election to UP's Student Council as part of a ticket headed by law school classmate Macapanton "Jun" Abbas, Jr. While Jun loses, I win a very narrow margin and am elected to the position of university councilor!

Jun may not have captured the hearts and minds of UP's students, but he certainly did a masterful job when it comes to winning my heart and mind! A brilliant debater and eloquent speaker who has Chinese facial features, Jun possesses one of the sharpest minds within our Law Class of 1967 cohort. Without setting out to, he's created stirrings within me that I didn't know existed.

I wonder if he has any clue my heart dances to an exciting new rhythm whenever he comes around? The same feelings are being felt by three of my girlfriends who are just as mesmerized by Jun's gravitas, wit, and charm as I am.

But Jun has a fatal flaw in my book: He's a devout Muslim who dreams of creating a Moslem state within the Philippines. Even so, there will always be a special place in my heart for Jun, because who doesn't remember their first crush? Plus, I've been broadened by befriending someone of the Islamic faith.

However, due to my Catholic faith, I don't think I could enter into a serious relationship with a Muslim, and I'm pretty sure Jun would never marry a non-Muslim unless she first converted to Islam. Be that as it may, the butterflies and sweaty palms I experienced in Jun's presence were interesting, to say the least.

Not long after our bid for student government posts, US President Lyndon Johnson travels to the US Embassy in Manila on October 24, 1966, to meet with Philippines President Ferdinand Marcos. Johnson wants the Philippines to send a battalion of soldiers to Vietnam so he can assure the world that the United States isn't fighting the Vietcong alone.

Sadly, and predictably, the Philippines Congress agrees to go along with this warmongering foolishness. Why put Filipino lives at risk to support Johnson, whose country couldn't give a hoot about the Philippines or its people? The UP Student Council decides to organize a student rally in front of the Philippines Congress building in Manila, with yours truly raring to serve my country by speaking truth to power.

The sun is shining brilliantly as our buses arrive in front of Congress to unload hundreds of students. Once the rally starts, hordes of animated and vocal—but otherwise orderly—students mass just outside the main gate, yelling uproariously as we wave placards protesting the servile, puppet-like actions of our Congress.

Gazing in the direction of the building's main entrance, I can't believe my eyes: For some reason, an arrogant-looking, uniformed Manila police officer is slowly unholstering his gun, which he then aims at the students protesting in front of him. What in heaven's name is wrong with this man?

Without thinking, I slowly stride over to where he's standing and gently place my right hand over the hand he's clutching his firearm with. "Sir, please put that down!" I tell him, struggling to modulate my voice so that I can still be heard, while at the same time not come off as aggressive.

"Sir, there is no need for that gun. This is a peaceful rally. None of us are armed."

As if he can hear my fervent, silent praying, the glowering cop slowly lowers his weapon and returns it to his holster, to the relief of wary students carefully monitoring our tense exchange.

My foray into politics continues during my remaining time in law school. During my final year, I run a UP Student Council re-election campaign. I vie for a position as a university councilor again and win convincingly, as does my close friend Violeta Calvo, who's elected vice chair. Another classmate, Jejomar Binay—who'll eventually become vice president of the Philippines—is also voted in as a university councilor.

Fortunately, I graduate from the University of the Philippines College of Law with no additional law-enforcement run-ins and have the seventh-best grade point average among UP's 57 law graduates in 1967. I'm especially proud to be a member of the UP Law Review Board of Editors, an honor accorded to College of Law students viewed as the crème de la crème.

As I practically float across the University of the Philippines' commencement stage, my fixation with the Notre Dame de Vie Institute is a distant, if thoroughly pleasant, memory. It turns out I don't have to disappoint Papa with my chosen career: I am fully committed to becoming a lawyer now.

Once the hoopla associated with graduation day subsides, I join three other College of Law graduates in renting a house in Manila, so we can sequester ourselves while prepping for the Philippines bar exam. During that time, I give the obsessive side of my personality free rein and study like a maniac, which enables me to ace the bar exam the first time I take it.

## A New York Minute

After watching me take the oath the Philippines Supreme Court gives to new attorneys, Papa is practically vibrating with joy in July 1968 as his eldest daughter achieves his dream of becoming a lawyer.

As a reward, he promises to send me and Mama on a worldwide tour after I'm admitted to the bar, to include stops in Honolulu, Los Angeles, San Francisco, Las Vegas, Chicago, Washington, D.C., and finally New York City, where my sister Mely is earning a graduate degree from Columbia University.

After visiting Manhattan, Mama, Mely, and I are to tour Europe, before I return to Manila to work as a corporate lawyer for Papa's business conglomerate. Once that's under my belt, Papa says we'll hatch a plan to launch my political career in Sorsogon.

Mama and I touch down at New York's Kennedy Airport in September 1968 and excitedly take in the sights of New York City from inside a cab taking us to the Aberdeen Hotel, a 12-story apartment hotel at 17 West 32nd Street in Manhattan. Mely is staying with us at the Aberdeen, where we'll share a cramped one-bedroom unit with a stove and refrigerator.

If the thought of three affluent women cramming themselves into a teeny room sounds odd, the Nicolas family is frugal, as I've noted. Anyway, I got plenty of practice with communal living while growing up in the Philippines. Every summer, my family visited a resort in

Baguio City, where 14 of my first cousins and I would be in one room on straw mats placed on the floor. By comparison, being in a hotel room with only my mother and sister feels downright luxurious.

After I splash some water on my face in our hotel bathroom, Mama, Mely, and I leave the Aberdeen to do a tiny bit of sightseeing before the sun sets. The three of us are euphoric as we saunter shoulder-to-shoulder past storied Broadway theaters that are within walking distance of the Aberdeen. "Watch out—here come the Nicolases!" Mely laughingly calls out to no one in particular as we saunter down the sidewalk. In time it will be clear that New York City should have been warning us, instead of the other way around.

Prior to visiting, I'd seen so many movies and read so many books featuring Manhattan that I felt I knew it quite well. But after a couple of days spent strolling through Central Park and gawking at preposterously tall skyscrapers, it's clear that I don't know Manhattan at all. I had also mistakenly thought that my earlier visit to Chicago would provide an excellent yardstick for dealing with the Big Apple. Not even close.

New York City is . . . a high-voltage cauldron of sights, sounds, and smells that engage and stimulate the brain like no other destination on earth. The teeming humanity here and the city's electric aura are equal parts exhilarating and overwhelming. I secretly admire Mely for how effortlessly she seems to have adapted to Manhattan since becoming a Columbia University graduate student.

For a theater lover like me who acted in my high school and college plays, New York City is the stuff of dreams. Mely, bless her heart, knows of a place that sells deeply discounted tickets for Broadway and off-Broadway shows. I take full advantage of that connection as Mama and I lavish tourism dollars on New York City's economy, while waiting for Columbia's winter break to end Mely's classes. To my horror, the spending money I brought with me disappears "in a New York minute," as folks here love to say.

## THE "MEET CUTE"

Mama and I decide to remain in Manhattan until Mely gets her degree in May 1969, so I need to get a job. Mama is flush with cash thanks to the prospering pharmacy she owns back home in the Philippines, but the Nicolas kids know better than to approach our well-off parents with outstretched hands. That's a no-no as long as we're able-bodied.

Given that I speak fairly fluent—if heavily-accented—English, I start looking for work in order to support my Great White Way musical addiction. My search leads to an employment ad in the *Village Voice* alternative weekly newspaper, where an unnamed employer is seeking an "administrative assistant in a civil rights research council."

I can do that! I constantly conducted legal research in law school, and I'm still looking to support just causes, even if I'm not a nun. So, I mail a cover letter to an address that appeared in the *Village Voice* ad. Because I suspect I'm overqualified, instead of disclosing that I have a law degree, I tell a little white lie that I'm a second-year law student at the University of the Philippines.

A lie of any kind—white, black, or in between—is considered a sin by Catholics, so as I say my prayers that night at the Aberdeen Hotel, I tack on an Our Father and ask for God's forgiveness. It must have been granted, because a few days later I'm asked to interview for the civil rights position.

The interview takes place in an office in the Chelsea section of Manhattan, and my inquisitor is a tall, handsome African American Harvard Law graduate Reynaldo Glover, executive director of Law Students Civil Rights Research Council. I happen to be a terrible liar and am secretly relieved when "Rey" doesn't ask a single question about my educational status.

I guess I make a good impression because he hires me on the spot. I'm to come to the research council's offices Monday through Friday, and my hours are 9 to 5, at a regal $150 per week. I'm rich!

Fortunately for me, I took a typing class at St. Theresa's College, even though it wasn't a requirement to graduate. God helps those who help themselves.

I hightail it back to the Aberdeen Hotel, where Mama and Mely are as thrilled as I am after I tell them about my good fortune and my new boss. Because Papa never catalogued people based on skin color or economic status, I don't mention that Rey is Black. That's not to say that colorism isn't a big thing back home in the Philippines—it's a *huge* thing. When I was growing up, individuals who were *Mestizas*, meaning they were half-White in appearance, were considered gorgeous. Filipinos are generally very prejudiced when it comes to skin color and just can't seem to shake the racist viewpoints of our Spanish and American colonizers. A surefire path to wealth in the Philippines would be to create a new and improved version of the popular skin-whitening creams sold throughout the country.

After working with Rey for a few weeks, I get a sense that my intellectual, independent-minded sister might enjoy meeting him. Mely and Mama already feel like they know him because I'm always returning to the Aberdeen Hotel with stories about the insightful and humorous observations constantly flowing from Rey's mouth.

"Mely, let me introduce you to him," I suggest to my sister, who's currently working as an office temp, something she'll stop doing after Columbia's spring semester cranks up.

The next day, Mely comes to my office, and I introduce her to Rey. They hit it off immediately, to the point where they've scheduled a date for this coming weekend.

Wow, my boss works fast!

On Friday, Rey drops by my desk as I'm filing documents, answering the phone and firming up his schedule for the following week. I glance up, curious what new task he's about to lay on me.

"Loida, how would you like to go on a double date with Mely and me tomorrow?" he asks, catching me off guard. For one thing, 99% of what he discusses in the office tends to be work-related. Also, even though I'm 25, I've never been on a date!

"Sure! Why not?" I quickly reply with what I hope doesn't sound like an abundance of eagerness.

"Beautiful. I'll pass the details to Mely," Rey says with a Chesire Cat grin. Has Mely blabbed that her devout big sister is floating along in a cloistered, date-free little universe? Who is Rey going to pair me with? And what, exactly, have I gotten myself into?

Good Lord!

Rey sashays into his office, before returning about 5 minutes later. "It's all set. His name is Reginald Lewis, and he was one of my class-mates at Harvard Law.

"You'll like Reg," Rey says on the way back to his office. "He's cool."

I have to admit that I'm intrigued. An attorney who's attended the best law school in the United States will probably be smart as a whip, highly verbal, and incredibly driven.

Sounds like someone I know.

After getting dolled up in two of our nicest dresses, topped off with perfume and the tiniest hint of makeup, Mely and I head to the Aberdeen Hotel's lobby to meet Rey and this Reginald Lewis character. Even though I know she's probably dying to take in the spectacle, Mama remains in our room after telling her daughters to have fun and stay safe.

As Mely and I check each other out a final time in the elevator, I'm feeling calm, even a little blasé, about my upcoming encounter. I'd thought I might be a little nervous in the run-up to my first date, but for me it's the same as when I used to accompany my female and male University of the Philippines College of Law classmates to dinner.

Neither Rey nor Reginald is present when Mely and I hit the lobby, so we both grab a seat on a couch facing toward the lobby door. We keep our coats on, because December 7 in Manhattan feels a lot harsher and unwelcoming than it does in the Philippines, where nighttime lows are usually around 75 degrees this time of year.

Within a minute or two, Rey and Reginald make their way into the lobby. I immediately notice that Reginald is two or three inches shorter than Rey, who's roughly 6 foot 1. While not unattractive, Reginald isn't as handsome as Rey, but from the way his business suit fits him, I can tell Reginald is on the muscular side.

Moving with a tightly coiled, debonair grace, he practically saunters across the Aberdeen lobby as he approaches me to shake my hand. His handshake is firm, although not overly so, a mistake some men fool-ishly make when meeting a woman for the first time.

"I'm Reginald Lewis," he says in a steady, deep voice as he locks his piercing, dark eyes onto mine. "Very nice to meet you."

"I'm Loida. I have heard so much about you!" This is my standard opening whenever I met a new acquaintance. However, it appears to flatter Reginald, who shoots a delighted smile that exposes a gap between his two front teeth, along with cute dimples in his cheeks.

Rey and his friend help Mely and me to our feet, a sign of good home training. But when we walk out the front door and Reginald grabs my left elbow, I'm caught off guard. In the Catholic-centric, conservative Philippines, men and women who don't know each other definitely do not touch.

So Reginald's move to steady me as we leave the Aberdeen Hotel strikes me as "fresh"!

It's only 22 degrees outside as we double daters quickly walk toward Rey's car, an impressive-looking red Ford Mustang that's parked on the street. Reginald and I enter first and sit in the back, with Mely in the front passenger seat and Rey driving. I'm overjoyed the car starts on the first try, because I'm ready for the Mustang's heater to get going.

As we start rolling down Seventh Avenue, Reginald turns to me with an impish smile and says: "Today is my birthday."

"Really? Then, happy birthday!"

"Don't I get a kiss?" he demands playfully.

Seeing that my initial read of "fresh" was on the money, I oblige and give Reginald a peck on the cheek.

"How sweet!" he exclaims, clearly delighted that we haven't been in Rey's car for 10 minutes before Reginald finds out what my lips feel like.

As soon as Rey's car finally get comfortably warm, we're pulling in front of Boondocks Restaurant, at Tenth Avenue and 15th Street in the East Village. A Black-run establishment that serves soul food, Boondocks has sawdust on the floor and James Brown's *Say It Loud!* booming from the jukebox.

As we're being seated, I wonder if Rey and Reginald know that Boondocks is an Americanization of the Tagalog word *bundok*, or mountain? Boondocks was introduced into the American lexicon by G.I.s who'd served in the Philippines from 1898 to 1946. Wondering if I'll sound hopelessly nerdy by introducing this, I err on the side of caution and keep it to myself.

When a waitress drops off four menus at our table, I'm surprised to learn that soul food shares a lot of similarities with Filipino cuisine. Therefore, I feel comfortable ordering ham hocks, while Mely, Reginald, and Rey opt for fried chicken.

In the Philippines, pork is considered fare for the wealthy. In a country that's surrounded by water, ordinary people eat dried fish, while pork is considered a delicacy. It feels funny to be in an eatery where anyone can pop in, order pork chops, and think nothing of it.

When our drink orders are taken, instead of asking for something pedestrian like soda or beer, Reginald orders an entire bottle of champagne, which impresses me to no end!

As the evening progresses, Reginald and I embark on a wide-ranging conversation that ping-pongs between topics—until, that is, I ask him what it's like to be a Black man in America.

"I'm international!" he informs me forcefully. "I don't encourage or embrace labels that allow people to pigeonhole me."

He doesn't want me dealing with him as a Black man, but as a human being. So just like that, he erases the concept of race from our conversation, which impresses me further.

Finding our meeting of the minds tremendously enjoyable, once we're back at the Aberdeen Hotel, I thank Reginald for taking the time to meet with me, Mely, and Ray, and I wish him continued success with his legal career.

## THE SECOND DATE AND GOOD-BYE

A few days later, the phone in my hotel room rings, and Mama motions for me to pick it up. It's Reginald.

"Would you like to join me for dinner on Saturday?" he asks quietly.

Thoroughly elated, because I really did enjoy his company during our first meeting, I agree without hesitation.

For a second Saturday night it's brutally cold outside, prompting me to put a pair of thin shorts over my underwear. Atop the extra insulation, I don a dress that I typically wear to work. After Mama and Mely approve of my fashion choice, I enjoy a wonderful dinner with Reginald at a Greenwich Village restaurant that has a Spanish decor.

As before, I'm impressed when he orders a bottle of champagne, which he practically puts away singlehandedly, since I have only one glass.

Tonight, much of our conversation is dominated by a riveting excursion Reginald took from Boston to Europe the summer after his first year at Harvard Law. He proudly recalls how he flew on a chartered plane that only charged a $200 round-trip fare for his awareness-raising, 30-day journey.

"I met a Netherlands art student named Helge Strufe who was in Paris on a limited budget, so I invited him to share my hotel room," Reginald relates casually, as if people do that sort of thing every day. "Helge told me that when I reached the Amsterdam leg of my trip, to give him a call.

"When I reached Amsterdam, I stayed in his apartment, where Helge's watercolors were hanging on the walls and strewn all over the place."

Impressed by his friend's prolific output and noting that he needed help marketing his art, Reginald modestly relates how he arrived at a solution.

"I volunteered to sell his watercolors at the Harvard COOP bookstore, if he mailed them to me from Amsterdam. Helge did that, and his art sold very well. The pieces I wasn't able to move now hang on the walls of my apartment."

Noting that I'm clearly transfixed by his generous, adventuresome nature, Reginald inquires: "Would you like to see them?"

Would someone who's earned an undergrad degree in humanities like to see art created by Reginald's friend? Absolutely. Plus, I'm curious what the apartment of a young American lawyer looks like.

"Sure, that would be nice."

After dinner ends and Reginald has taken care of the tab, we brave the frigid night air to catch a taxi to 333 West 21 Street, a Chelsea address where my date lives alone in a minuscule, fifth-floor walk-up apartment. The unit consists only of a kitchen area, a tiny bathroom and an ultra-compact living room, where Reginald has a small bed, a sofa for two, and a long table that's laden with stereo equipment, as well as framed art by his friend, Helge Strufe.

Reginald looks admiringly at the watercolors, which are abstracts with strong primary colors of red, orange, blue, green, and black. I'm so relieved the paintings aren't hideous, because my penchant for telling the truth sometimes causes me to utter the first thing that pops into my head.

"These are really nice," I state simply. "I see why you were drawn to his art."

"What can I tell you, Loida?" he laughs. "I have an eye for beauty."

With practiced ease, Reginald turns on his stereo and starts playing a record by Frank Sinatra. We sit on Reginald's sofa, which is so small that we're very close to each other.

As Sinatra croons in the background, Reginald smoothly positions his left hand behind my waist and pulls me closer. I don't object, because I'm starting to like this straightforward, sophisticated, entrepreneurial, cerebral man. Nor am I surprised when Reginald starts lightly kissing my lips—if anything, I'm surprised how much I enjoy it!

As our kissing becomes more passionate, I'm not the least bit alarmed, because what we're doing in the privacy of Reginald's place couldn't feel more natural. Or pleasurable.

It's only after he scoops me up in one motion and begins carrying me toward his bed that shrieking alarm bells go off.

"No, no, no," I cry out in a panicky voice. "No!"

As someone who's only entered the dating game a few days shy of my 26th birthday, it suddenly dawns on me how naive I was to agree to come to Reginald's apartment by myself. Only now am I realizing that I entered into a tacit agreement to be intimate with this man.

C'mon, Loida!

Reginald becomes a perfect gentleman the second he realizes I'm feeling imperiled. "I just wanted to touch you," he says, sounding despondent as he goes off to fetch our winter coats. "I would *never* do anything you don't want me to do."

During our taxi ride back to the Aberdeen Hotel, an awkward silence envelops the vehicle. Neither of us would mind if the cabbie started zipping through the streets at 100 mph, allowing us to put this night behind us as quickly as possible.

To Reginald's credit, when we arrive at the Aberdeen, he gently, courteously opens the taxi door for me and then accompanies me into the lobby, where he bids me good night.

Because it would reflect poorly on Reginald, as well as on me, I don't tell Mely or Mama what transpired in Reginald's apartment.

The next day, I take a ballpoint pen and some paper down to the Aberdeen Hotel's lobby and write Reginald a quick letter:

> Dear Reginald,
> I have enjoyed talking to you because we have many things in common. It was fun being with you. But I do not want to see you again. I shall only have intimate relations with the man who will be my husband. However, I shall remember you with fond memories.
> Sincerely,
> Loida Nicolas

Don't ask me why, but when I place my letter in an envelope, put a stamp on it, and drop the letter into a mailbox near the Aberdeen Hotel's front entrance, I feel a palpable sense of relief.

# 3

# "I HAVE A HEADACHE!"

**M**en love to snicker about women being hopelessly "addicted" to gossip. Not only is that a classic example of the pot calling the kettle black, I'd bet two Broadway theater tickets that Rey Glover knows all about my horrible date with Reginald Lewis last weekend.

I mean, come on, they're best friends. But whenever I steal a glance at Rey's face while we're at work, nothing in his expression indicates he's thinking about anything beyond our next Law Students Civil Rights Research Council staff meeting, or the fresh cup of coffee I've just placed on his desk.

His decorum enables me to gradually push Reginald Lewis to the margins of my memory and concentrate on what's really important: enjoying Mama and Mely during our New York City adventure, executing top-notch work for Rey, and tracking down particularly noteworthy Broadway and off-Broadway theater productions.

## MR. PERSISTENT

To my surprise, one afternoon in the middle of the week, I answer my ringing desk phone and whose voice should come booming through the line but Reginald's!

Did the postal carriers suddenly go on strike or something, because surely he got my letter? And it sure would be nice if someone invented a phone that indicates who's calling before you answer it!

"Loida, I'm at my law firm, so I can't stay on long," he says without a hint of embarrassment, shame, or trepidation, as I stare at my phone in disbelief. What planet is this guy from?

"But if you don't have plans, I was curious if you'd like to join me Friday for dinner?"

I feel like there are only two clear-cut options at my disposal—hang up or say "yes." Clearly, there's no way he's read my letter, so . . .

"I can meet with you on Friday, Reginald. What restaurant did you have in mind?"

"One of Manhattan's best. It's a surprise, but I'm pretty sure you'll like it. I'll drop by the Aberdeen's lobby at 7. And Loida?"

"Yes?"

"Thanks for going out with me."

And with that, Mister Persistent is gone. I keep holding the phone as my brain attempts to unpack what's just happened, but my head is being canceled out by the warm, mushy feelings starting to blossom in my heart.

The site of our next date is Max's Kansas City, a trendy restaurant and nightclub on Park Avenue South that's frequented by celebrities and jetsetters. Dinner delivers more of what Reginald and I greedily feasted on during our previous meals: scintillating conversation that reveals how two people who couldn't appear more different actually embrace surprisingly similar worldviews.

I learn more about Reginald's background; during his earliest years he was raised in Baltimore by a single mother who left Reginald's father when Reginald was five; his grandfather Sam Cooper served the United States Army in France during World War I; Reginald was a football star at Baltimore's Dunbar High School and went to Virginia State University before he was admitted to Harvard Law School.

To augment my conversational main course, I order lobster at Max's Kansas City, marking the first time I've eaten the seafood delicacy. It's wonderful! Reginald watches intently as I dig around in the shell, searching for morsels of sweet white lobster meat. Noticing his fascination, I inquire why he didn't order lobster too.

"Oh, no," he says, with a chuckle and a vigorous shake of his head. "Too much work!"

After we've savored dessert and Reginald is walking me into the lobby of the Aberdeen Hotel, I'm unable to keep my raging curiosity in check a second longer.

"Did you know I wrote you a letter?"

"Yes, you did."

Not sure I heard what I thought I just heard, I do a double-take. "I wrote you that I never want to see you again. So why did you call me?"

"Loida, I will never do anything you don't want me to do."

He's got a point there. Because it would have been a simple matter to reject his Max's Kansas City invitation. I could easily have hung up the phone the instant I recognized his voice.

Just as I could have passed up the opportunity to warmly embrace Reginald in the lobby of the Aberdeen, right before he hails a cab back to his apartment. But I do hug him, and doggone if his solid, well-toned body doesn't feel right at home in my arms.

As Mama and Mely sleep comfortably in our hotel room later that night, I lay awake in bed, observing how the headlights of vehicles passing the Aberdeen are casting eerie shadows on the ceiling. Making a desperate effort not to toss and turn, I order my brain to stop whirring, demand that it stop fixating on Reginald Francis Lewis. Even though I've never encountered this situation before, I see it for what it is: If Reginald and I continue to see each other, I'm going to fall in love with him.

That would make zero sense, because after Mely graduates from Columbia University, I'm leaving Manhattan for the Philippines, never to return.

Still . . . it wouldn't hurt to get a second opinion about the strange place I'm currently in. Ideally, from someone with a brutally frank way of cutting to the chase whenever I seek her counsel: Josefina Opeña.

Jo-pie and I were close friends at St. Theresa's College, where she graduated summa cum laude. Open-minded, liberal, intellectual, and glib, Jo-pie's currently in Manhattan attending Fordham University, where she's working on a doctorate in child education.

Jo-pie has a White boyfriend, John Disterhoft, that I know she's sleeping with, even though she has her own apartment. So, I give her a call.

"Jo-pie, I am getting attracted to Reggie and if I continue to see him, I am afraid I'll end up sleeping with him," I confide.

"And? So, what? What's wrong with that?" Jo-pie shoots back.

"Didn't the Catholic sisters say no sex before marriage?"

"Fuck the sisters—they don't know anything," Jo-pie says, causing me to wince. She knows full well that profanity makes my skin crawl, but that doesn't keep her from spewing foul, sulfurous words into my ears. "The physical act is just a natural manifestation of what you feel for one another," Jo-pie says in a somewhat gentler tone. "And anything that's natural comes from God."

Well, that settles it.

## BECOMING MORE INTIMATE

Reginald is unlike any man I've ever met. I'm incredibly driven, tenacious, and ambitious, and to meet someone who surpasses me in every regard is amazing. If we begin to date steadily, I realize that a "natural manifestation" is inevitable. But not only am I okay with that, I actually welcome it.

However, I quickly discover that Reginald has been married from the moment we met. Not to a woman, but to his job as a corporate attorney at Paul, Weiss, Rifkind, Wharton & Garrison, a top Manhattan firm.

The two of us often go to dinner after my workday ends at the Law Students Civil Rights Research Council. Once we're finished eating, I head back to the Aberdeen Hotel, while Reginald returns to Paul, Weiss, where he thinks nothing of putting in 12-hour days.

I've seen this act before—Reginald is a younger version of Papa, except he lives in New York City and has a Harvard Law degree. Both men feel compelled to outwork the competition, a mindset I share, but not to the degree they do. The world contains way too many captivating activities and places for me to devote 12 hours a day to a vocation, day in and day out.

Not surprisingly, the first time I make love to Reginald, it takes place in his apartment. I'm beyond terrified, but Reginald's so patient and gentle that he makes it a terrifically pleasurable experience for both of us.

Reginald is a tremendous lover who's slowly chipping away the puritanical facets of my personality. Along with showing me how to enjoy strip poker, something I would never have considered a year ago, he's teaching me to be comfortable in my own skin. There's nothing inherently sinful about the human body, Reginald's or mine.

He's also giving me a wonderful music education with the Bose stereo equipment in his apartment. Aided by a glass of champagne and a cigar, he relaxes while enjoying records by opera singer Maria Callas, Lena Horne, Shirley Bassie, Aretha Franklin, Nat King Cole, and Sammy Davis. And of course, Frank Sinatra, who was playing during the ill-fated seduction attempt we now get a huge chuckle out of.

Mely and Rey are also boyfriend and girlfriend now and seem to have a very active love life of their own, if the frequency of Mely's late-night arrivals to the Aberdeen Hotel is any indication. One weekend night she tip-toes into our room around midnight, as Mama and I are sleeping. When Mama hears the door slowly opening, she instantly sits bolt upright in bed.

"Where have you been?"

"With Rey."

"Did you sleep with him?"

I cringe upon hearing this. Mama, you're hitting waaaay too close to home.

"Yes," Mely replies without hesitation, in keeping with her M.O.

Enraged, my mother throws such a massive fit that I'm hoping she doesn't have a nervous breakdown! I lay still in the bed, trying magically to become invisible, and praying Mama doesn't have the temerity to ask if I'm sleeping with Reginald. Because she'll be totally undone if she learns her goody-two-shoes daughter is also cavorting in Manhattan. But after receiving the shock of a lifetime from Mely, I guess Mama decides discretion is the better part of valor and slips out of inqui-sition mode.

If you don't want the answer, don't ask!

Rey is booted a little further into Mama's doghouse. She was already annoyed with my boss after Rey playfully shoved Mely into a snow-bank, causing her to catch a bad cold afterward. Reginald, on the other hand, is good as gold with my mother. She's a tremendous fan of his seriousness and industriousness. Plus, she probably can't envision Reginald getting intimate with the daughter who came within a whisker of becoming a nun.

A few days prior to Christmas 1968, with the world transfixed by the saga of three US astronauts orbiting the moon for the first time, Reginald gets a wicked head cold. It's so bad that he cancels plans to drive to Baltimore, where he was going to spend the holiday with his mother, Carolyn Fugett, and the rest of his family.

After pushing his trip back, he calls me on December 26 to find out if I'm interested in dinner. We wind up going to the Mark Twain's Riverboat Restaurant, a jazz spot that's in the basement of the fabled Empire State Building and that serves as a venue for world-renowned big bands. Which is something I know zilch about.

"Count Basie and his band are playing tonight," a nearly breathless Reginald relates as soon as we reach Mark Twain's Riverboat. I don't have a clue who Count Basie is, whether he's a singer or what, but I can tell from Reginald's enthusiasm that this Count guy is a really big deal.

Fact is, I didn't really come to the Empire State Building to hear music, or even have a meal. Something else is weighing heavily on my mind. My boyfriend and I need to have an important talk.

We're seated at a table that's close to the restaurant's vast dance floor and that affords us an excellent view of Count Basie. Our dinner is hardly memorable, just basic American fare. And as always, Reginald orders a bottle of champagne to wash down his food.

When we're finished eating, Reginald asks if I'd like to hit the dance floor, which I have no problem with. He takes my hand, and we sashay to the music of Count Basie Orchestra, which strikes my untrained ears as somewhat stately.

Moving in perfect rhythm with my first and only love, I lean in so that my mouth is nearly level with his left ear.

"Reggie, I think we should stop seeing each other."

"What? Why?" he asks, caught off guard by a verbal sucker punch that Count Basie provided a live soundtrack for.

"I am falling in love with you, and you probably feel the same way about me," I tell him, immensely relieved to finally get this off my chest. I don't deal in subtext; I don't like leaving important matters unsaid and festering out of sight. Except when I'm lying in bed beside my mother as she harangues Mely about her sex life.

"I do not want to break my heart, and yours too, because I am going back to the Philippines," I tell Reginald. This isn't a warning or a threat, but a simple statement of fact. I'm not into ultimatums or childish stuff like that, I'm just laying out facts, as we were both taught to do in law school.

"How do you know?" Reginald replies gently. "You really don't know what will happen."

I have no comeback for that, because he's absolutely right. How do I know? He's basically telling me to wait and see how things play out, which makes sense. I can live with that approach. Now that I've said what I needed to say, my conscience is clear.

Afterward, instead of tapping the brakes, we accelerate our emotional entanglement by beginning to see each other even more frequently. It's a move that seems to suit both of us.

Reginald loves movies, mostly action films, so on weekends we spend quite a bit of time snuggling in darkened theaters. When we're on his turf, namely, his fifth-floor Chelsea man cave, I do my best to learn the ins and outs of cooking fried chicken, while faithfully following one of his mother's recipes.

Not only was my man a star quarterback at his Baltimore high school, but he also earned an undergraduate football scholarship before getting injured. Football strikes me as a typically American pastime, which is to say it's overwrought, brutish, and regarded as if it's larger than life. However, when your sweetheart spends Sundays gleefully soaking up professional football, when in Rome, do as the Romans do.

I'm patiently taught why it's the end all and be all when a team scores a touchdown and learn to differentiate between a quarterback and a tight end. To my everlasting surprise, I'm starting to enjoy watching games with Reginald . . . but will probably never watch a single minute of the game when he's not present.

Falling in love hasn't caused Loida to totally disappear!

As we get more and more in sync with one another's rhythms and sensibilities, the calendar indicates that Easter is a week away. Reginald suggests that we spend Easter on the Caribbean island of St. Thomas, which is part of the US Virgin Islands.

I originally thought this was solely his idea but come to learn that the attorneys at his law firm have a custom of heading to the Caribbean for Easter. What do Americans call this—keeping up with the Joneses? Whatever the correct phrase is, I never pictured an independent thinker like Reginald ever following a crowd. But on the other hand, I'm really looking forward to spending time in St. Thomas with him.

One of Reginald's Harvard Law classmates lives in St. Thomas, so I tell Mama I'll be staying in the classmate's house, in a guestroom. Another white lie . . . but Mama would have had a heart attack if she learned I'll be sharing a hotel room with my boyfriend.

I purchase two plane tickets to St. Thomas on an airline that has the cheapest fare available, courtesy of a stopover in Puerto Rico, and also because the flight departs New York at midnight.

Rather than wait for midnight to arrive inside Reginald's apartment, I suggest that we take in a Broadway play, because he hasn't seen one since starting his job in Manhattan last year.

In frugal Nicolas fashion, I buy two of the cheapest tickets to "Man of La Mancha," a musical that's currently the hottest play on Broadway, and we lug our bags to the theater.

Despite being in nosebleed balcony seats that makes onstage actors look like singing, dancing ants, Reginald is mesmerized by *Man of La Mancha,* especially its signature song, "The Impossible Dream." Which strikes me as apt because my boyfriend continually talks about using entrepreneurship to become "the richest Black man in America!"

Anyway, since I've taken the time to learn a new lexicon that contains terms such as "first and goal" and "backfield in motion," it seems only fair that I should get a theater partner out of the deal.

Exhilarated following a standing ovation and several curtain calls, Reginald and I grab our bags and catch a taxi to Kennedy Airport for our jaunt to St. Thomas. In Puerto Rico, we trade a comfortable, roomy jetliner for a rickety propeller plane that takes us the rest of the way to St. Thomas, where we enjoy five idyllic days in Charlotte Amalie, the capital.

It feels wonderful to turn off my brain and simply be free of thinking that includes, "how do you characterize this relationship?" and "what's our next step going to be?" But after I return to New York City, those same thoughts ambush me as soon as we get back into our work routines.

One night as we're seated in an empty subway car, I turn to Reginald with a half-smile on my face. "Darling, would you want a small wedding or a big wedding?"

"A small wedding," he replies without hesitation.

"Where do you think we should have it?"

"At New York University's chapel . . ."

Suddenly realizing what we're discussing, Reginald places a hand against his forehead.

"I have a headache," he says.

"Darling!"

Laughing joyfully, I give Reginald a kiss on the cheek. The ball is in motion.

## A SECOND GOOD-BYE

In the days and weeks that come on the heels of my "engagement," Mely earns her graduate degree from Columbia University.

Mama had returned to the Philippines in March, two months earlier, after an import/export business she tried to start in New York City fizzled. Plus, things were uncomfortably tense between her and Mely, following the late-night episode involving Rey.

As for me, well, I'm falling back into my bad habit of overthinking things to the nth degree, specifically, the implications of marrying Reginald and then living in the United States. During quiet moments, I mull what it would be like to leave the Philippines, my family, and friends for good. Not to mention Papa's dream of me pursuing a political career.

No question about it, I have cold feet, and they're growing icier by the day. To the point where I wind up calling Reginald at his law firm during one of my lunch breaks at the Law Students Civil Rights Research Council. My heart is pounding so hard that I'm certain Rey is politely pretending not to hear it.

Reginald gets on the line sounding vaguely irritated, which isn't uncommon when he's at his office.

"Reginald, I cannot go through with our wedding. I'm sorry." Rather than try to intervene, he quietly listens, waiting for the source of my angst to appear. From my tone, he can tell that my mind is made up, so any attempt to dissuade me would merely waste his time.

I knew he would basically wish me luck and wouldn't stoop to begging, which is just how things play out before the call ends. I hang up with a leaden lump in the pit of my stomach: Have I just managed to make the dumbest decision of my entire life?

After canceling our plans to visit Europe, Mely and I book a flight to the West Coast to visit friends enrolled in graduate programs at Stanford University, in Palo Alto, California. Afterward, the plan is to touch down in Seoul, Taiwan, and Hong Kong, before ending our journey in Manila.

My sister and I want the ultimate memento for our return to the Philippines, namely, Rey Glover's red Mustang. Having decided that it's too expensive to own a car in Manhattan, Rey's selling his vehicle to us for $600.

There's only one problem, which is that my sister and I don't have $600 in cash. I try to think of some folks I know in New York who might be willing to extend a short-term loan. My good friend Jo-pie can't do it because she's a student right now . . . maybe Reginald Lewis can?

Primarily looking for an excuse to see Reginald one more time, I drop by the offices of Paul, Weiss, Rifkind, Wharton & Garrison and am greeted by my ex-fiancé—or is it ex-boyfriend—who coolly, cordially and firmly lets me know that it's his personal policy not to lend money to anyone.

I couldn't care less; my objective was to see him before leaving the United States, a move that I now see was a terrible one any way you cut it, although I admire him for standing firm on a matter of principle. Years later, I'll learn that Reginald's mother characterized my actions that day as "ruthless."

In the end, Papa comes to the rescue by sending $600, plus what it costs to ship the Mustang to Manila. On June 9, 1969, Mely and I fly from New York to San Francisco, on what's probably the most pain-filled transcontinental flight of all time. At 30,000 feet it hits me that I'm never going to see Reginald again, leading to a gloom that follows me across the United States and dogs my every step after Mely and I land in San Francisco and catch a bus to visit our friends at Stanford.

## Back Together, Forever

After reaching a point where I can't endure another second of this wretched lovesickness, I give in and place a long-distance phone call to my beloved in Manhattan.

His personal phone rings once, twice, three times, and my heart sinks a little with each unanswered ring, before he finally comes on, sounding like he doesn't have a care in the world.

"Hello?"

I close my eyes, relishing the sound of a deep, commanding voice that I want to wake up to for the rest of my life.

"Darling, I am coming back!"

I guess Reginald knows me better than I thought because he doesn't sound at all angry or vengeful. Everything—our conversation and even our pet names we have for one another—is exactly as it was before I flew to California.

"Since you're already on your way home, tell your parents about our plans," Reginald suggests. "Then you can come back to New York, we'll get married, and we'll fly to Paris for our honeymoon."

When I tell Mely about the call, she gives me a huge bear hug, relieved to be rid of the moping, catatonic traveling partner who'd highjacked her big sister's body.

With my wedding plans back on, I do something that's uncharacteristically cowardly: I write my friends in Manila and ask them to inform Mama and Papa of my plans to marry Reginald F. Lewis, whom Mama has already met. I ideally should convey this news myself, but hide behind my pals and let them prepare my parents for the big shift in their eldest daughter's future.

When Mely and I are finished with our travels and finally make it back to the Philippines, I show Papa a photo of Reginald that was taken while we were in St. Thomas. Papa takes one look at Reginald in his swim trunks, looking virile, dynamic, and raring to take on the world, and he immediately gets it. Papa doesn't say anything, but I'm sure he saw a younger version of himself.

My mother's brother, Uncle Pedro Mañalac, who's visiting, comes up with an interesting idea: "Why not get married here, instead of New York? That way, Reginald can see you in your environment and get to know your family, relatives, and friends."

So, once again I find myself tentatively reaching out to Reginald via long-distance, not at all sure how my uncle's suggestion will be received. I needn't have worried because the thought of flying 10,000 miles to claim his bride instantly appeals to my future husband's sense of adventure and romance.

## THE BIG DAY

"Loida. Loida! Time to get up, *anak* (child)."

It's 4 a.m. on Saturday, August 19, 1969, as Mama gently nudges me awake in my bedroom. It's my day of days, with my nuptials to Reginald Francis Lewis scheduled to begin in three hours, so the punishing midday, equatorial sun can't abuse the 300 or so guests expected to attend.

My father booked Reginald in the Manila Hotel, where the wedding reception is taking place. I hear he's been having fun in Manila with my uncles, nephews, and brothers, where he's reportedly drinking all comers under the table with ease. Boys will be boys, regardless of nationality. Or, for that matter, age.

It's still dark outside as I come bounding out of bed like a jack-in-the-box, eager to dive into a day that can't possibly feel any more surreal than it already does. A hairdresser follows Mama into my room, followed by a makeup artist. After they work their magic, I don a magnificent hand-embroidered wedding gown and float down the stairway of the house we now live in, which is located in Makati City, part of metropolitan Manila.

Accompanied by Mely, who's my maid of honor, and my youngest brother Francis, who's my best man, and Mama and Papa, we hop into a car that our driver, Pascual, guides to St. Pancratius Chapel, located in Manila's picturesque Paco district.

A circular structure that has beautiful Romanesque architecture and a domed roof, St. Pancratius Chapel isn't air conditioned. Another reason my wedding, which will be officiated by Catholic Sorsogon cleric, Monsignor Florencio Yllana, is starting at 7 a.m.

My wedding planner, Dennis Mendoza, clearly knows his business, because my wedding comes off without a hitch. Before I'm able to grasp what's happened, I'm Mrs. Reginald Lewis and find myself schmoozing with hundreds of wedding guests during a reception inside the Champagne Room at the Manila Hotel. Our wedding cake is a replica of the Empire State Building.

Me, the prudish bookworm who was going to be a nun is now Mrs. Lewis! I keep grinning at Reginald, the man I'm going to the United States with to begin a new life. He's looking somewhat gobsmacked himself, but not to the degree that I am.

I feel like I'm on a movie set, and this entire event is unreal. Did this really happen? As Reginald smiles at well-wishers, and we go from table to table to greet my classmates and friends and my parents' friends, it dawns on me that my life as Mrs. Reginald F. Lewis is starting.

# 4

# DRAGONS AND MONSTERS

After our wedding, one of the first things Reginald and I do as husband and wife is scurry off to Manila International Airport to catch a Philippines Airlines flight. Mama comes with us to the airport and silently cries her eyes out the entire time, which makes my heart ache.

"Promise me you will take care of Loida," she says to Reginald between sobs, causing tears to slide down my own cheeks.

My new spouse, who's slipped out of his tuxedo and into casual vacation clothes, firmly grasps my mother's hands and looks directly into her eyes with a loving smile on his rugged face. "Please do not worry," he says in a reassuring voice. "I'll take care of her."

I didn't know it, but Reginald had already secretly promised Papa that he would send me back to the Philippines at least once a year to visit my family. My spouse can be sharp-tongued and hot-headed at times, among other faults, but he's always kind and respectful toward my parents, which is one of the many reasons why I love him.

When our jetliner roars from a Manila International Airport runway for the four-hour journey to Japan, I'm incredibly sad to be leaving my kinfolk and my homeland, but tremendously excited to be starting a new life with the most dynamic person I've ever met. This feels right—at 26, I have no doubt God has paired me with my soulmate.

I scoot over in my narrow airline seat and rest my head on Reginald's rock-solid shoulder. Both of us are so tired from the hours-long ordeal of taking pictures and dancing and shaking hands at our wedding that we quickly fall asleep.

Our honeymoon in Tokyo and the ancient city of Kyoto is marked by three nights of memorable passion, in part because we've been apart for two long months.

During the day, we have fun going through the Ginza section of Tokyo, one of the city's top shopping districts. Then we move on to Kyoto, an ancient city whose ebb and flow is several centuries behind Tokyo's. In Kyoto, we stay in a Japanese inn called the Ryokan. Instead of a bed, we sleep on a mat in a room that has a hot tub and that's visited by a geisha who scrubs our backs with warm water. Very Japanese.

The two of us are running around Japan having mastered exactly one word of the native language—*sayonara*, meaning "goodbye." Not real useful when we're trying to order in a restaurant or are asking directions, but we get by through relying on pantomime and by flashing yen when necessary. When two people are head-over-heels, there's not much they can't conquer together, including language barriers.

Kyoto doesn't have a big shopping area like Tokyo, but that doesn't keep me and Reginald from buying something we treasure throughout our marriage, namely, a beautiful woodblock print by famous Japanese artist Utagawa Hiroshige.

During the Japanese leg of our honeymoon, Reginald confides that while he was in Manhattan prior to our marriage, he deeply resented the fact that I changed our wedding plans.

"You know what saved you?" he tells me matter-of-factly. "I received a letter from you every day!" Fortunately, I'd had the presence of mind to write him while we were separated in order to keep the fires burning.

Good thing, too, because Reginald says that after his flight from New York City landed in Hong Kong, a flight attendant came on the intercom and said: "Those proceeding to Paris, please stay onboard. Those going to Manila, please get off for your connecting flight."

For an instant Reginald mulled staying in his seat and jetting off to Paris, his favorite city and a place his grandpa, Sam Cooper, had come to relish while serving in the US Army during World War I. As a boy, Reginald heard story after story from his grandfather about how the French had treated Black American soldiers with admiration and respect. Not only that, but Reginald had visited Paris himself while on a summer break from Harvard Law School and had a fantastic time.

But as he sat in his airline seat in Hong Kong and envisioned me standing alone at the altar in Manila—jilted, heartbroken, and utterly humiliated—he says the temptation to head to Paris instantly disappeared. He hopped off the plane, went into the airport terminal, and found the gate for his connecting flight to Manila. As he was destined to.

## THE HONEYMOON IS OVER

The second part of our honeymoon plays out in Honolulu, where I get a rude awakening at Honolulu's airport. Things go awry as soon as I present my Philippine passport and a US tourist visa to an immigration officer. He looks over my visa and casually inquires, "How long are you staying in the USA?"

"Permanently," I answer truthfully. "I just got married."

Oops. Wrong thing to say. Seems tourist visas are for those merely visiting the United States, not for people intending to stay permanently. I'm separated from Reginald, who has a US passport, and am escorted to a part of the airport set aside for immigration investigations. Naturally Reginald's puzzled and very concerned as to why I'm being led away instead of being allowed to go through customs with him. And is it my imagination, or does he appear to be seething as I walk away?

No question that I'm alarmed because I'm being separated from my new husband and because I'm not sure what these dour-looking immigration people have in mind. I'm led to a little room, the door is closed behind me, and an immigration officer begins an interrogation! He keeps asking about the US Embassy in Manila, where my tourist visa was issued. If I knew I was getting married to an American, he wants to know, then why did I request a tourist visa? Am I on the up and up or trying to hide something?

Starting to feel somewhat uneasy, even though I've done nothing wrong, I calmly tell the immigration official for the third time that I never went to the US Embassy in Manila. Papa's travel agent handled the details of my trip back to New York City, including securing my tourist visa.

For the longest time the immigration official simply stares at me and says nothing. I stare back, not with defiance, but with an expression that makes it clear I feel power is being abused. My interrogation finally ends and I'm "paroled" into the United States, pending an appearance at an Immigration and Naturalization Service office located in Manhattan at 26 Federal Plaza.

Bureaucracy being what it is, it will take another year before I'm finally granted the status of a permanent resident married to an American citizen. My unsettling run-in with America's immigration system plants a seed: If I manage to pass the New York bar exam, I'm definitely going to become an immigration lawyer!

Honolulu marks a turning point in my honeymoon. In Japan, Reginald and I were two high-spirited newlyweds enjoying life to the maximum. But the smile he flashed the entire time we were in Japan fails to make it out of Honolulu's airport terminal. Reginald heatedly claims I was only singled out for additional Immigration and Naturalization Service (INS) screening because I was with an African American.

I'm not sure what he means by that, but I do know there's no way I'm going to let INS ruin my honeymoon!

Hawaii is a popular vacation destination for White Americans in 1969, and as we encounter them Reginald repeatedly grumbles that "those crackers" are doing and saying things that telegraph their bigotry. However, I don't see what Reginald is seeing, which further enrages my sensitive, proud spouse.

In his opinion, the racism he's observing stems from the fact that we're an "interracial couple." Maybe I'm naive, but I don't view us that way. It never occurs to me to monitor how others are reacting to us, because aren't we just two people in love? For me, the only other person in Honolulu is Reginald F. Lewis. I'm with the man I love, so I'm totally focused on what he's doing, saying and feeling.

But whatever he's picking up is causing him to become increasingly agitated as we spend a day touring the city. It takes only about 24 hours for Reginald to get his fill of Honolulu—he cuts our honeymoon short and arranges for us to head back to the airport for a flight to New York City! If someone drew a cartoon of us, a black cloud shooting yellow lightning bolts would be over our heads, and Reginald would have a huge scowl plastered on his face.

This is the first time I've seen him react to US race relations in such a dramatic way, and his irritation is putting a damper on our honeymoon. However, during the long flight to New York he relaxes, and his anger at the White Americans we met in Honolulu dissipates. As such, I'm thrilled to be returning to New York as Mrs. Reginald Lewis and am excited about our future together.

## SUSMARIOSEP!

My new home in Manhattan is what New Yorkers call a "railroad apartment," meaning the tiny rooms are directly connected and there are no hallways. This is quite a change from my family's expansive home in the Philippines, where hired help routinely tackles cooking and cleaning chores. But I'm happy nonetheless. The way I see it, creature comforts are irrelevant when God has blessed you with the love of your life.

The two of us are in a fifth-floor walkup located at 333 West 21st Street. It probably takes 30 seconds to stroll through our entire place, which has a big room in the front that overlooks the street, a kitchen, and a small room that's supposed to be a bedroom, even though we use it more as a study.

Reginald and I sleep in the living room, where a bed has been positioned beside the wall and a couch sits in front of the window. There's also a long wooden table that holds a very expensive Bose stereo system, Reginald's first significant purchase as a lawyer.

Needless to say, we don't do a lot of entertaining in our small place.

Our first year as a married couple is tough. For one thing, I'm thoroughly lost in a kitchen—the only things I've mastered are boiling rice and making scrambled eggs. To Reginald's credit he lovingly, patiently, teaches me how to cook pork chops, hamburgers, and steaks. I try really, really hard, but apparently his cooking lessons aren't sinking in as he had hoped. One day when I'm not around, he calls his mother, Carolyn Fugett, in Baltimore and complains: "Mom, Loida cannot cook a hamburger right to save her life!!!"

"She was not trained to cook," Mom accurately informs my husband, who replies: "You have a point!" Afterward, Mom doesn't hear any more carping about my meager cooking abilities. To be honest, Reginald's critique of my hamburger-cooking skills catches me off guard—I was under the impression that steaks were what I always screwed up, not hamburgers!

Mom kindly passes along her recipe for fried chicken, and to my delight, I quickly become Manhattan's top chicken-frying Filipina. Being told that my fried chicken is "close" to Reginald's mother's is the highest praise imaginable.

Aware that housecleaning also isn't a strength of mine, Reginald hires a cleaning woman who comes by every two weeks to tidy up our railroad apartment. There's so little space and so few possessions, I can't imagine it would take more than 15 minutes to get things in order. I keep that observation to myself and simply let the cleaning woman do her thing, because that's what I'm used to in the Philippines.

At least I manage to keep our apartment decorated with fresh flowers. In the months leading up to my wedding I took a course on creating Ikebana Japanese floral arrangements because I figured Reginald would appreciate having pretty flowers around our home.

But food and flowers aren't the big sources of tension in our marriage. The main problem is Reginald's temper. I had no idea how frequently, and intensely, it erupts. So I try putting myself in his shoes and come to the conclusion that being a Black man in a racist society means he's always being unfairly prejudged. I'm guessing that creates pressure that manifests itself as anger and rotten moods.

As I first observed in Honolulu, my man flares up at the slightest hint of prejudice and discrimination. This also holds true at the Manhattan law firm where he works, Paul, Weiss, Rifkind, Wharton & Garrison. A secretary there who reflexively addresses White attorneys as Mr. Korman and Mr. Schumer made the mistake of calling my spouse Reggie, and he lopped her head off. Reginald was still enraged by the time he got home, which has gotten to be a distressingly common occurrence. The way I find out is by making an innocuous comment that somehow triggers a thunderous argument!

Making these confrontations even worse, oh God, is the cursing. S-O-B! The words flying out of his mouth when he's enraged sprinkle salt on my wounds. F-U-C-K! He knows I don't curse—I think it's an American thing. S-H-I-T! I can't stand it. The closest I get to saying bad words when I'm angry is muttering "*Susmariosep,*" a shortened form of "Jesus, Mary and Joseph!"

The profanity is an expression of Reginald's frustration, but bad language was never a habit of mine growing up. To me, it's like clothes—there are just certain clothes you don't wear.

When I was a girl back in the Philippines, I promised myself that if ever I got married, I would never have ugly scenes in my house the way Papa and Mama sometimes did. They'd walk around huffing and shouting at the other, with each having a different interpretation of what the other just said.

However, now I'm a wife who appears to be heading down the same conflict-laden path my parents traveled. For me, things reach a low point after he comes home one night fired up over some work-related slight. He glares at me with those intimidating, deep-set eyes of his and disparagingly growls, "You don't know where I live!"

In other words, I don't know what his innermost desire is; I have no clue what's motivating him to act, to move, to work like a man possessed. Given that I consider myself highly empathetic, "You don't know where I live!" stabs me in the heart, because it means I've somehow overlooked something.

Moving forward, I begin employing silence as a weapon when Reginald and I have words. I keep my lips sealed, even when I believe

I'm right and he's dead wrong. But in my head, I go at my husband word-for-word, which increases his annoyance.

"I know what that silence means," he lets me know in a booming voice. "That's aggressive silence!"

*Susmariosep!*

Although I have the self-discipline to not voice my emotions, my eyes betray me by unleashing torrents of tears. Whenever he sees me crying, Reginald cuts his harangues short. Afterward, he never comes back and formally apologizes for his outbursts, but does and says little things that indicate he's remorseful.

Here's how I've come to view our dynamic: My husband's out in the world fighting the dragons and monsters of racism, bigotry, and discrimination, and when he comes home, he should not find another dragon or monster waiting for him.

His status as a junior Paul, Weiss attorney often causes Reginald to show up at our apartment late at night, after hustling for business. Instead of confronting him with, "Where have you been?!" I instead ask, "Darling, have you eaten?"

And whenever he appears stressed and worn out, I'll hit him with: "Darling, do you want a massage?" I make it clear that whatever our circumstances, he can always depend on getting 110% of my love and fidelity.

And should he ever find that's not enough, I've let Reginald know that he's free to walk out the door, because I can take care of myself without him.

I live for the weekends, when all of Reginald's time isn't devoured by Paul, Weiss. On Saturdays and Sundays, I have better odds of running into the man who charmed me into spending the rest of my life with him. Weekends are for acting like newlyweds, for gawking at Manhattan's myriad attractions, and for going to movie theaters.

Reginald loves movies, whereas I'm more attracted to Broadway and its amazing plays. But cinema is the cheaper option, so we'll share a bucket of popcorn and watch things like *Casablanca* and *Butch Cassidy and the Sundance Kid.*

With Paul, Weiss out of the picture, my husband is far more tender and affectionate in his approach to me, including our lovemaking. On weekends, there's no doubt in my mind that he loves me. But when the weekend ends, I know the dragons and monsters aren't far off.

I knew Reginald had a temper when we were courting. He was authentic—there was no falseness in him. I knew of his shortcomings as I was falling in love with him, but now that we're married, I see those faults with newfound clarity. Plus, he's unveiled a new one I didn't know about—jealousy.

I discover this when he takes me to a gala associated with his work at Paul, Weiss. We dance together a couple of times, a rare treat for both of us, and are sitting at our table when one of Reginald's colleagues asks if I'd like to hit the dance floor. Not particularly, but it would be rude of me to say no, so I dance to one song and return to my table.

After Reginald and I leave the gala, he's irate because he feels I was flirting with my dance partner. And I just can't get him to understand that I'm naturally friendly and don't care one whit about whomever he's jealous of.

So, the next time we're out dancing, I only dance with Reginald, and I look at him the entire time. No one else but him, so there will be no quarrels after we get home. I'm aware Reginald's mother left his father when he was 5, which may have put abandonment worries in his subconscious. But I've already told him several times, in no uncertain terms, that I will never leave him.

## MY DEVOTION TO MY MARRIAGE

Midway through our first year as man and wife, I find that Reginald's moody, confrontational ways have worn me to a nub. I simply can't take any more.

Unable to communicate with my husband and unwilling to expose my turmoil to Mama, my sister Mely, or my close friends, I pick up the phone in our apartment and hesitantly dial a long-distance number. I'll hang up if the phone rings more than three times, but a strong, reassuring presence comes across the line after only two rings.

"Hello?"

"Hi, Mom . . . it's Loida." I thought that hearing her voice might be unsettling but in my exasperated state, nothing has ever sounded better in my entire life. "Mom, he is really difficult!" With anyone else, I'd have to recap what prompted that comment, but Carolyn Fugett is probably more familiar with Reginald's obstinate, fiery ways than anyone. I do share, however, that it may be time for me and her son to go our separate ways.

"I understand, Loida," Mom calmly replies, as if we discuss things like this all the time. "I'll put this on the altar. There's no rush, so give it some thought, okay honey?"

"Thank you, Mom. I will."

"Did he make you listen to ugly words?" We both know the answer—Reginald always fires off epithets whenever he's angry.

"He did," I sigh. "Yes."

"Tell you what—go in the bathroom, spit in the toilet and flush it," Mom advises, as if she intuitively knows I keep unspoken comments bottled up in my head.

After I hang up, I go and spit into the toilet of my railroad apartment. And I flush the toilet. And I calm down.

Reginald's temper, gutter mouth, and false accusations haven't diminished my love for him one bit. And I have every intention of seeing our marriage through.

Manhattan is full of street vendors who sell inexpensive art, especially near the famous art museums on Fifth Avenue. One weekend afternoon as we're admiring drawings and paintings sprawled across the sidewalk, Reginald sees a piece of artwork he just has to have.

Drawn in black ink over a white background is an unlucky soul whose head is being squeezed by a massive vise. "That is how I feel," Reginald says matter-of-factly, pointing at the distraught-looking Black man in the picture.

I understand, Darling. I understand.

# 5

# LOVER/MOTHER/ LAWYER

After a few months of marriage to Reginald, I feel as though I could enter the Boston Marathon and utterly destroy the competition. And I don't mean just the women's category; I'm talking about the entire field!

I'm easily in the best shape of my life because our five-story walk-up apartment in Chelsea has no elevator. There's no avoiding a narrow, steeply inclined stairway every single time I leave our apartment or every single time I return. I keep telling myself that I'm going to count the stairs one of these days, but when you're huffing and puffing up a wooden mountain to retrieve a forgotten letter that you meant to mail, getting an accurate accounting of your steps quickly becomes an afterthought.

My life these days seems to be an interconnected series of gantlets, with the intimidating staircase fitting nicely into the larger picture. I'm also navigating my new marriage to a prickly, highly ambitious mate, while acclimating myself to the biggest city of a global superpower whose rhythms and sensibilities couldn't be more alien to someone from a little Philippines town.

The most curious thing about life in the United States is just when you feel you've got it figured out, you get a curveball that leaves you flailing and feeling totally mystified. One of these curveballs is tossed my way in a supermarket around the corner from our apartment, while searching for items I forgot during a previous visit.

After locating what I'm looking for, I casually walk to one of the cashier lines and wait. As I mentally map out the dinner I'm about to prepare, out of the blue a woman's voice bellows: "You CHINK!"

Huh?

It takes a moment for my brain to comprehend that this person could be referring to me, because folks of every stripe call New York City home—Dominicans, Chinese, Italians, Ethiopians, East Indians, Greeks. One of the things I love about this place is its insane diversity. I'm not saying New Yorkers give each other heartfelt hugs on the street, but "CHINK"?

I turn to find an elderly White woman glaring at me, her face contorted with rage. Where's this coming from—does she know me from somewhere?

"Wow!" I tell her, surprised I'm able to verbalize my thoughts in the face of such eye-popping racism. "You're using a racial slur!"

"Goddamned right!" the woman shouts, her features scrunched into a constipated-looking grimace. "You saw me standing there, but you cut in front of me anyway."

Feeling like my face is ablaze, I slowly turn back around. I did not cut in front of her! But what could I possibly say to someone so hopelessly ignorant and small-minded? How can a stranger's facial characteristics or skin color generate such fiercely negative emotions in her?

After making my purchase and hurriedly leaving the supermarket, I amble down the sidewalk and try to process what's just happened. But I cannot. Whichever way I analyze it, the encounter just keeps defying logic.

America can be a complex, at times bewildering, place to live, but I'll never fully understand the racial tapestry here. The way that tribal hostilities and resentments are always bubbling just beneath the surface amazes and saddens me.

The entire world is buzzing over the technical know-how and bravery that deposited Neil Armstrong on the lunar surface a few months ago, and it views the United States as the greatest country on earth. But how much greater could it be if it fully unleashed the wisdom and talent of all of its citizens?

That evening, I don't mention my supermarket run-in to Reginald. I already know how incensed he would be and don't wish to add to the burden he carries. Still, the supermarket clash gives me a small window into what my man experiences as an African American.

After spending our first year of marriage in a claustrophobic man cave, my husband and I move into the London Terrace apartment complex on 460 West 24th Street. For $200 a month, we get a proper 14th-floor, one-bedroom that has huge closet spaces. Most of all, London Terrace has an elevator! I secretly chuckle that I deserve to be awarded some kind of medal or certificate to show that I survived a year of running up and down the five-story stairway at 333 West 21st Street.

## Starting a Firm

Like some other newlyweds we know, we didn't mesh terrifically well during our first year of marriage, but the wise counsel I received from Reginald's mother proved invaluable. Now that he and I are more in sync and have more square footage to work with, it's not surprising that we occasionally talk about the possibility of starting a family.

This relieves me to no end because I have married girlfriends who discovered after walking down the aisle that their men didn't want children. Reginald and I agreed before marriage that we both did, and it's great to hear that reaffirmed now that I have a ring on my finger. We're not ready to start trying just yet, but we agree kids are definitely on the horizon.

Reginald doesn't realize it, but he's helping me make another major decision, namely, that I never want to work for a major Manhattan law firm—or a small one, for that matter.

They treat young associate lawyers like Reginald as if work, aka billable hours, should be their be-all and end-all.

Paul, Weiss is one of Manhattan's top business law firms, and Reginald intends to gain as much legal expertise from the place as he can, prior to starting his own law practice. And that is precisely what he does in 1970, co-founding the first African American law firm on Wall Street, along with attorneys Fred Wallace, Rita Murphy, and Josephine Thorpe.

Wallace, Murphy, Thorpe, and Lewis' first year of operation is partially funded by the National Urban Coalition, an organization formed in 1967 in response to racial unrest in major US cities. But most of the money flowing into the firm's coffers results from Reginald's hustle, unrelenting work ethic, and impressive business contacts. He's out cultivating potential clients just about every night.

When we privately discuss his law partners, it doesn't sound as though they possess Reginald's burning determination to outwork his peers. We both foresee them eventually falling by the wayside, with the law firm becoming solely Reginald's. He's hard-nosed under ordinary circumstances but especially so when he feels—correctly or incorrectly—that someone isn't pulling their weight in a work setting.

When Reginald eventually winds up the last man standing at his Wall Street firm, I'm not surprised. While his approach is more direct, confrontational, and caustic than mine will ever be, water always seeks its level, as they say.

The many ways that Reginald and Papa are kindred spirits is downright eerie. They both have a habit of dreaming big and then executing tenaciously. Thanks to them, I have little desire to pursue wealth personally, because I'm always doing it vicariously, especially with Reginald, who's exponentially growing my knowledge of business, particularly finance. Could it be he's doing that intentionally?

## NOT STARTING A FAMILY JUST YET

One Saturday morning when he's working at his law firm, Reginald's secretary calls to let my husband know she's contracted German measles. We instantly realize this means Reginald may have been exposed to the virus, which health officials say increases the odds of pregnant women delivering babies with birth defects.

My regular OB-GYN, Dr. Robert Berke, is on vacation, so I go to another physician and get a German measles vaccination shot in my left arm. Dr. Berke isn't happy to learn of this after he returns and warns Reginald and me not to conceive within the next three months, due to the German measles vaccine in my bloodstream.

As luck would have it, I accidentally get pregnant inside the three-month window, turning what should be an incredibly joyous occasion into one full of anxiety, stress, and profound sadness. Reginald and I pay a visit to Dr. Berke, and he lays out two stark options: we can let my pregnancy go to term, or I can have an abortion. Even though he never says so explicitly, I can tell from the inflection in my OB-GYN's voice that abortion would be his choice.

My husband squeezes my hand as my eyes fill with tears and a weird coldness begins circulating throughout my body. Dr. Berke's lips continue to move, but I can no longer hear a thing he's saying. I can only think of the beautiful, innocent child Reginald and I have made and how our baby doesn't deserve to be in this predicament.

We don't make an immediate decision at Dr. Berke's, but after we get home and wait a day or two for the shock to wear off, my beloved and I decide that abortion is the best course of action.

Back in the Philippines, Papa has been insistently inquiring when my husband and I will make him a *lolo*, Tagalog for grandfather. I tell my dad in a tear-stained letter that his grandparenting days won't be coming any time soon, because I need to do something that definitely runs counter to the Catholic Church's teachings.

I don't want to bring a deformed child into the world, and I don't want to take a potentially heartbreaking gamble when there's zero doubt I've been exposed to the German measles virus.

Please forgive me, Lord.

After the procedure, my husband and I are down in the dumps for weeks. We just drop off the radar without telling our friends the reason behind our abrupt disappearances. Unless someone has had the misfortune of experiencing an abortion, they can't begin to fathom the intense sadness, anger, and depression that results.

Our shared tragedy draws Reginald and I closer, but at a horrific cost.

We'd both like to get away from Manhattan for a spell, but Reginald is working night and day to stabilize his fledgling law firm, and I haven't earned any vacation days from a secretarial job I've taken with Manhattan Legal Services on East 116th Street in East Harlem, which is a Puerto Rican community. The brainchild of the late Senator Robert Kennedy, Manhattan Legal Services is federally funded and represents impoverished city residents in administrative law cases dealing with landlord/tenant issues, unemployment insurance, and Social Security, among other things.

About a year after my wedding, I saw a newspaper ad for the Manhattan Legal Services position and found the prospect of helping poor East Harlemites very attractive. I expected a thumbs-down from Reginald, because in his family, when wives stay home as homemakers, that's a powerful statement that the man of the house is prospering. I'm relieved to find he's a lot more progressive than some of his male kinfolk.

"Sure, go for it!" he breezily advises me. "You're an independent, capable woman, so why the hell not? I don't give a damn what my relatives say about what happens in our house."

I had told Reginald that since he typically represents well-heeled clients as a corporate lawyer, it would be good if I could help Manhattan Legal Services represent the poor.

Why a secretarial job? Because I'm not cleared to practice law in New York—I haven't taken the New York State bar examination. In fact, the bar has a prohibition against administering the test to applicants who aren't US citizens. But after I'm hired, Manhattan Legal Services Executive Director Emilio Javier starts giving me cases he ordinarily assigns to lawyers. Not only does he see that I'm capable of handling the responsibility, but I'm also fluent in Spanish, which obviously comes in handy in a predominantly Puerto Rican neighborhood.

By the time January 1973 rolls around, my Manhattan Legal Services salary is equal to what the organization's new lawyers are getting paid. But fortunately, I have to quit—I'm pregnant again, and my due date is next month!

## Becoming a Family

My first clue something was up was linked to a crazy desire for lobster that materialized out of nowhere. No morning sickness, just a constant urge to head over to El Quijote, a Spanish restaurant beside the Chelsea Hotel. Reginald and I found it hilarious that I blew off all of El Quijote's wonderful culinary concoctions in favor of the $4.95 lobster dish on the menu.

Ever since Dr. Berke verified the source of my craving, which made me the scourge of the lobster world during my first trimester, Reginald has been an attentive, doting teddy bear who's significantly ratcheted back his salty language. As was the case with my father, Reginald just knows he and I are having a girl, who he's already named Leslie. My beloved says that years down the road, when our daughter mails an application or a résumé, she won't have to contend with the sexist viewpoints that feminine first names automatically conjure up. Makes sense to me.

With my dutiful husband by my side, I attend Lamaze classes so I can have my baby naturally, but without excruciating pain or anesthesia. My pregnancy unfolds without incident until Saturday, February 10, 1973, at 2 a.m. . . . is that sporadic pain what I think it is? I gently rub Reginald's shoulder to awaken him.

"Darling. It is time!"

He immediately pops out of our bed as if spring-loaded and proclaims: "Oh my God! Let's be calm!" I'll laugh about this endlessly in years to come, but in the midst of labor contractions, Bob Hope and Richard Pryor together couldn't coax a smile out of me.

Abuzz with excitement, but managing to remain collected and unfrazzled, Reginald flies out of our London Terrace apartment and hails a cab that carries us to Beth Israel Hospital, where I give birth to Leslie four hours later. Kudos to Lamaze, which works exactly as advertised, because I do not experience incapacitating pain.

Reginald's demeanor and support are peerless for the most part, but cracks start showing in his façade around the three-hour mark. Before I'm wheeled into the labor room, my beloved husband is alarmed by how red my face has gotten from exertion, so he starts belligerently lashing out at one of the nurses.

"Darling, please, don't scream at the nurse," I plead with my over-zealous protector. "You're upsetting me!" He quiets down after that.

After gorgeous Leslie Lourdes Nicolas Lewis is gingerly placed on my hospital bed, she fixes her unblinking dark eyes on my face as if to ask, "Are you my mother?" I do the most appropriate thing you can do after nurturing and incubating another human being inside you for the better part of a year, and then sharing your hidden treasure in the scariest way imaginable—I thank God over and over again.

Throughout my life, whenever I've had to master a new body of knowledge, my M.O. has always been to cram and cram and then cram some more. I study new challenges into submission, grind them into dust, but that's not how it works with parenting. You have to trust your instincts, read Dr. Spock's *Baby and Child Care* book, and muddle your way through.

But parenting always comes with a wildcard—your child. She may be a compliant conformist who's eager to please, like I was. Or she could be supremely strong-willed and interested in figuring out life with minimal interference, which describes my beautiful daughter to a tee.

Long before her second birthday, it's clear to Reginald and me that Leslie is a brilliant, artistic soul who's determined to move through the world based on her rhythms and no one else's. This throws me for a loop, because my childhood was spent around strong-willed Filipino mothers who made their children cede to their wishes. Or else.

I'm a hyper-achiever who always masters new things with ease, so it frustrates me that Leslie often has me wrapped around her finger, instead of the other way around. Sweet and loving when things are unfolding according to her plans, Leslie is already demonstrating noteworthy linguistic ability.

When I introduce her to smatterings of Tagalog, my baby picks up the language effortlessly. Which is why she'll instantly stop what she's doing and glance at me warily after hearing me say, "*Walang hiya na batang Ito. Papaluin ko ikaw!*" Which Tagalog speakers know is, "You have no shame. I will spank you!"

When Reginald wants my daughter's undivided attention, he merely utters a deep-voiced "Leslie!" and our strong-willed child magically heeds her father. As I say, frustrating, but by and large I'm enjoying motherhood. The tender moments easily outnumber the challenging ones, and the three of us are bonding nicely as a family.

## BEING TESTED, AS A MOTHER AND A LAWYER

Having his own law firm has enabled Reginald to seize a co-counsel position on a big New York City development project. The resulting fee brings an end to apartment life for the two of us, because in 1973 we purchase a massive five-story brownstone at 351 West 22nd Street for $120,000. I don't care how much in love two people are—inhabiting an itty-bitty one-bedroom at the London Terrace apartment complex, along with an infant, gets to be a bit much after a while.

We move into our brownstone before Leslie's first birthday, and our new dwelling is configured so that it has a duplex on the ground floor as well as an adjoining triplex on the third, fourth, and fifth floors. My family and I reside in the duplex while we rent out the triplex to tenants, an arrangement that helps defray the cost of our mortgage.

One of the things I love most about our new place is that it has a study where Reginald can keep the work-related documents he's constantly bringing home. He reads that stuff late into the night the way other people read bestselling novels. My beloved's law firm is helping scores of minority businessmen to buy existing businesses, which Reginald says is teaching him everything he needs to know to eventually buy a company himself.

Along with being a year that brings me my firstborn as well as my first house, 1973 delivers a final huge gift before drawing to a close: the U.S. Supreme Court decides that being born in a different country can no longer disqualify someone from taking a state bar exam.

After hearing this wonderful news, I immediately apply to take the bar exam for New York, which recognizes the University of the Philippines College of Law as equivalent to US law schools.

But part of the New York exam focuses on trusts and estates law, which doesn't exist in the Philippines and isn't taught there. So I enroll in a bar-review course with an outfit known as the Practicing Law Institute.

Successfully studying for a bar exam calls for every ounce of your focus and determination, as Reginald already knows, having passed New York State's exam. I'll need some powerful allies to pull this off, starting with my husband. I ask what he thinks of Leslie staying with his mother in Baltimore from April to July, while I study in our quiet brownstone. I add that I won't be cooking meals as I'm studying, so we can order food from nearby restaurants or simply eat out.

Reginald has no problem with this, and neither does his saintly mother, who I always address as Mom. She has a golden touch when it comes to childrearing, having raised five children with Reginald's step-father Jean Fugett, a kind, understanding man who I find out decades later is secretly a cryptologist with the US Department of Defense in Washington D.C.

When Reginald and I travel from Manhattan to Baltimore and drop Leslie off, she peppers me with guilt-inducing glares and whimpers as her father and I are leaving.

"It's only temporary, Loida," Reginald says consolingly during the trip back north to New York City. "Stop beating yourself up—Leslie will be fine." Whether it's motherly intuition or what, I'm not as convinced as my beloved is.

For 14 hours a day, seven days a week, I sharpen one figurative sword after another so I can lay waste to the bar-review dragon. Along with attending classes at Practicing Law Institute, at home I practice generating written responses to sample New York bar review questions. My handwriting is so bad that it would rival any physician's, so I devote a fair amount of time to making my penmanship more legible.

Whenever I'm unable to wedge another sentence of New York State law into my brain, I call it quits and take a brief nap. I learned years ago that continuing to plod forward will be a waste of time because my comprehension won't be up to snuff.

I've absolutely, positively got to pass this thing on the first try and am not doing anything that might jeopardize my chances of succeeding.

When the two days in July arrive where I'm to sit for the New York bar at the New Yorker Hotel, I feel cautiously optimistic as I enter a room full of anxious, highly caffeinated test takers. When the two-day ordeal ends, I immediately replace my student hat with my mom hat and catch an Amtrak train from Penn Station in Manhattan to Baltimore.

I need to reclaim my precious child!

Upon reaching 2802 Mosher Street, a rowhouse in East Baltimore, I dash up the stairwell to a second-floor bedroom where 17-month-old Leslie is in her crib. She gazes up at her mother's outstretched arms and coldly avoids my touch as if I'm a total stranger, and a threatening one at that.

I feel like she's punched me in the stomach!

"Come to Mommy, sweetheart."

"No!"

"Come on, Leslie. Don't do that, baby."

"Nooooooooo!"

Mom comes upstairs to see what the commotion is all about. She scoops up Baby Leslie and talks to her in a reassuring, gentle way as I stand by, waiting to be reconnected with my child. After she spends a few minutes in Mom's arms, Leslie comes to me and we have a reunion that warms my heart.

"Thank you, Mom! Thank you, Leslie! Sorry I had to be away for three and a half months, baby, but we're reunited now."

Following what feels like years of waiting, December 20, 1974, finally shows up. It's the day the *New York Times* is to release test results for the bar exam I sat for. It's also the day *The Godfather Part II* is released to theaters, so Reginald and I see it in a Times Square theater not far from a newsstand where the *Times* is delivered at midnight.

We thoroughly enjoy the movie and jump into his parked car afterward for a quick jaunt to where the newspaper is sold. Reginald eagerly flips through his hot-off-the-press *New York Times*, and when he reaches the page that has exam results, starts looking for "Lewis, Loida." I hold my breath, praying that I've passed, because if I've failed, I don't want to imagine another three months of exile for Leslie and of intense study for me.

But it sure appears my name isn't there . . . oh no. Please! "Look under Nicolas hyphen Lewis," I suggest, starting to feel tinges of desperation. "That's the name I registered under for the bar review.

And there it is—Nicolas-Lewis, Loida—I have passed the New York bar exam, becoming the first Asian woman to pass without attending a US law school.

HOOOOOONK! HOOOOOONK! My grinning husband blows his car horn loud and long. Thank you, God, because now I don't have to take the exam again or risk incurring Leslie's wrath a second time.

During the ride to our Manhattan brownstone, my thoughts are on my father, the would-be attorney. Papa's assured me over and over that diligence and determination are transferrable and will lead to success whether I'm in the Philippines or the United States.

As I cradle a *New York Times* that has my name printed in it, it appears that Papa's assessment about the worldwide currency of hard work is right on the money.

# 6

# FIGHTING TYRANNY AND DISCRIMINATION

**W**ielding the combined might of the pen and the printing press, my sister Mely and I have declared war on the Philippine government. We're battling the corrupt regime of President Ferdinand Marcos through protest publications we're printing in the Philippines and the United States.

In response, Marcos sends his soldiers to my family's Philippine home at 3 a.m. to arrest Mely, who's subsequently imprisoned for half a year on trumped-up subversion charges.

Compounding my unease is the sound of my father's quiet weeping during our long-distance calls. Not usually overly emotional, Papa is worried sick about Mely's safety.

At night Reginald and I quietly lie in bed, wondering whether Marcos' lackies have finally grown weary of my sister's rebellious ways and have permanently silenced her, a fate that's befallen untold numbers of Filipino dissidents. So, I welcome the dawn of each day and the many distractions that come with it, including raising my new daughter, looking for employment as an attorney, and supporting the man running Wall Street's only Black-run law firm.

Last but not least, I spend my time publishing my anti-Marcos newsmagazine, which is why I appeared on Marcos' radar in the first place.

## GOING UP AGAINST THE PHILIPPINES GOVERNMENT

In 1972, the year before Leslie was born, the leader of the Philippines was wrapping up his second—and last—term as president, due to term limits. Instead of obeying the Philippine constitution and allowing Filipinos to elect his successor, Ferdinand Marcos falsely claimed that communists had attempted to assassinate his defense minister, Juan Ponce Enrile.

This ruse enabled Marcos to declare martial law and remain in power, stunning a country that had no clue its longest tenured president had been a dictator-in-waiting all along. Disbelieving Filipinos fully expect their country's main benefactor, the United States, to get Marcos in line after journalists, activists, and politicians critical of the government are rounded up and jailed. Either that, or they mysteriously disappear.

A few months before martial law began, my fearless sibling started an underground, anti-Marcos spoof publication that she named *Imelda's Monthly*, clever wordplay pegged to the name of First Lady Imelda Marcos.

Mirroring Mely's actions, in Manhattan I begin publishing *Ningas-Cogon*, an anti-martial law, anti-Marcos newsmagazine. My first editions feature devastatingly witty pieces that appeared in *Imelda's Monthly* and skillfully skewer President Ferdinand Marcos and First Lady Imelda Marcos.

To support *Ningas-Cogon*, I recruit a handful of like-minded New York City Filipinos who are good writers and editors. One, Nonoy Marcelo, is a top-notch editorial cartoonist. At least one evening a month, we congregate in the living room of my Manhattan brownstone to map out our upcoming edition. *Ningas-Cogon*, by the way, means "brush fire" in Tagalog. Brush fires are fast-moving and intense, which is exactly how I view my publication.

Publishing a monthly newsmagazine is an expensive endeavor, even though I'm running black-and-white photos to save money. I'm selling one-year subscriptions to *Ningas-Cogon*, which has 32 pages per edition and is mailed to readers, for $30. Many advertisers are leery of buying ads in what's basically a protest publication against a major US ally. I'm able to get some support from Filipino businesses in and around New York City, though that doesn't always cover my $1,500 monthly budget.

So, after taking a deep breath, I approach my entrepreneurial spouse. To Reginald's credit, he's not a tough sell, having seen firsthand the impact that Ferdinand Marcos' murderous power grab is having on the Philippines as well as on me and my family.

Whenever I fall short of my $1,500-per-edition target, my beloved generously chips in the remainder. That enables me to get the newsmagazine to a New Jersey print shop and then mail it to roughly 2,000 Filipino subscribers around the country, although most of *Ningas-Cogon*'s audience is in the Elmhurst and Jackson Heights sections of Queens.

## FIGHTING IS NOT WITHOUT MONETARY COSTS

Reginald's largesse might evaporate if he looked into our household budget, because I'm bouncing checks like mad! For whatever reason, my checkbook just refuses to balance.

While my man covers big-ticket stuff like the mortgage and doctor bills, buying groceries and keeping our phone turned on is my responsibility. I like to patronize a butcher shop not far from our brownstone, and when I write them a check for pork chops—one of Reginald's favorite meals—a few days later the house phone will ring. "Mrs. Lewis, your check came back for non-sufficient funds."

"I'm so sorry," I'll tell our butcher. "Would you mind depositing it again?" And then my check will bounce a second time, forcing me to have another red-faced phone conversation with the butcher, who's fortunately a friend. Eventually, though, things reach a point where he demands that my purchases be paid for with cash. No more Loida Lewis checks!

Reginald is fastidious, even persnickety, about finances and making sure things balance out to perfection, so I never let him find out about these conversations. He has no clue that I have a secret, a one-inch-high stack of checks stamped NSF (for "non-sufficient funds") from our butcher and our neighborhood supermarket.

If Reginald were to stumble across it, I'm sure that would lead to a very uncomfortable, one-sided "chat" about how our credit rating is in such horrible shape. Which would further ratchet up the pressure I'm already feeling from trying to master motherhood, stopping checks from bouncing, finding employment, propping up *Ningas-Cogon*, keeping tabs on my family's safety in the Philippines, etc., etc., etc.

The phone company is also part of the debt-collection chorus because long-distance calls to the Philippines aren't cheap. I'm constantly angling for extended credit plans that keep the phone from getting turned off. I've found that if I at least make a partial payment, that keeps my dial tone humming.

I can't wait to make a meaningful contribution to the Lewis family's coffers, and my prayers are finally answered in early 1975 when I start practicing law with the Antonio Martinez Law Office, located at 324 West 14th Street.

Martinez is a Dominican American whose firm specializes in immigration law. My focus, which mirrors that of two other attorneys in the firm, is on deportation and naturalization cases involving Latinos from the Dominican Republic, Mexico, and South America.

Before heading off to Martinez's bustling practice, I first feed Leslie breakfast and wait for her babysitter, Marcelina, to arrive. After catching the subway and getting off at the first stop, I enter the Antonio Martinez Law office at 8:30 a.m. to pick up the files for the cases I'm handling. Afterward, I head to 26th Federal Plaza, a 50-story courthouse complex located near City Hall, and then represent my clients before administrative immigration judges as well as immigration officers.

Doing Martinez Law's bidding doesn't even feel like work because I know how much I'm helping. I've seen firsthand how US bureaucrats make life difficult for immigrants from non-European countries. An added benefit of working with Latinos is that the bulk of our interactions take place in Spanish, which I've gotten fairly proficient at speaking and understanding, thanks to the three years I spent working for Manhattan Legal Services in East Harlem and my years at school.

Antonio Martinez knows I'm a young mother, so he is not surprised when I hustle out of his law firm promptly at 5 p.m. to get Leslie's babysitter off the clock; then I cook Filipino fare for me and my daughter. Reginald is rarely home before 10 p.m., so until then, I bathe Leslie and read her a bedtime story, then make phone calls about *Ningas-Cogon* matters.

When my weary beloved gets home, I cook him pork chops, steak, or fried chicken for dinner, or order veal cutlets from Scotty's Restaurant. After I listen to how his day went, we go to bed around midnight and renew the cycle the following morning. My existence is far from conventional, with every single day being jampacked, but I love it. Give me a day with scores of agenda items to check off, and I'm right in my element.

For some reason, I've always had this thing about pushing my body and mind to their absolute limit. It was true when I was in school and it's still the case now that I'm a young wife, mother, and lawyer.

## WARTIME COLLATERAL DAMAGE

On the publishing front, after I reach a point where several *Ningas-Cogon* editions have been printed, the Philippines Consulate in New York City sends me and my editorial board an ominous message: Our names have been blacklisted for travel back to the Philippines.

This rattles me to my core because who knows when a health crisis or an accident might necessitate a trip to the Philippines. Beyond that, no one wants to be prohibited from seeing immediate family members, especially given that I want Leslie to stay connected to her Filipino heritage.

Before we even have a chance to discuss things with each other, my *Ningas-Cogon* staff and I independently arrive at the same conclusion: We're not going to be intimidated. We started the newsmagazine to hold a light to Marcos' abuses, so how would it look if we shut down at the first sign of bullying from a tyrannical dictator thousands of miles away?

Therefore, we keep printing, but I need some kind of arrangement that'll let me safely visit the Philippines in the event of a family emergency. Everyone working with my newsmagazine is an immigrant, but seeking help from the Philippines Consulate isn't an option.

Reginald agrees to intercede and visits the consulate on my behalf. He tells me that a security man with conspicuous bulge under his suit jacket hovered nearby the entire time as Reginald got Ambassador Jose Pineda to agree that I can return to the Philippines without being apprehended.

In return, *Ningas-Cogon* has to let the Philippines Consulate run a news release or article in every edition. This works for me because I know *Ningas-Cogon*'s coverage of Ferdinand Marcos and his regime will remain hard-hitting.

Back in the Philippines, Mely has folded *Imelda's Monthly*. When she was arrested, Marcos' men went directly to where her printing equipment was hidden and confiscated it, a clear sign that *Imelda's Monthly* had a government informant in its ranks.

But here in Manhattan, I keep pumping out *Ningas-Cogon* on a monthly basis.

## Schooling Uncle Sam

In July 1975, I'm alerted that the US Immigration and Naturalization Service (INS) office in Manhattan has 11 attorney openings, so I eagerly apply. Not only would that allow me to try more complicated immigration cases, but working for the INS would result in better pay and benefits.

A month goes by without any word from the INS about my application. Then half a year. Then an entire year drops from the calendar before I finally get a brief letter that says I wasn't one of the 11 selectees. I get zero explanation as to why I was rejected or why it took a year to notify me.

I decide to hold the INS's feet to the fire and personally file a lawsuit accusing the agency of discrimination based on national origin, race, and gender. In keeping with the general tenor of things, after I file my suit it takes three ridiculously long years before an administrative hearing is finally scheduled for my case.

When my day in court arrives at long last, I testify before a judge that if he stacks my credentials and application against those of the 11 attorneys the INS ultimately hired, it will quickly be apparent I should have been chosen. Seeing the logic behind that argument, the judge orders the INS to send him the applications of the 11 lawyers the agency hired.

Following a wait of six more months, during which the INS blows off the judge's demand for the attorneys' employment documents, the judge rules in my favor. As a result, not only do I become an INS lawyer, I'm also awarded three years of back pay, two months' worth of vacation, and one month of combined sick leave and personal leave.

When I say goodbye to my colleagues at the Antonio Martinez Law Firm, the entire staff is genuinely sad to see me go because I have always vigorously represented the rights of those being processed through the US immigration system. On the other hand, Antonio Martinez and everyone are thrilled I'm becoming a federal immigration attorney because they know I'll keep right on fighting the good fight as a system insider.

On the home front, Reginald is suitably impressed by how I've taken on the mighty INS and defeated it by being strategic and unyielding. "Babe, go on with your bad self!" he says with a grin, prior to opening a bottle of Moet et Chandon to celebrate my victory.

In June 1979, the INS lets me know that I need to take a monthlong course at the U.S. Citizenship and Immigration Services Academy Training Center, in Glynco, Georgia. Oh noooo—my thoughts immediately flash back to the three months I spent away from Leslie to study for the bar review and how deeply resentful she was afterward.

Reginald suggests that it might be less disruptive if his mother comes to Manhattan this time, instead of uprooting Leslie and sending her down to Baltimore again.

So once again I find myself making a long-distance call to Mom, to see if this time she's willing to come to Manhattan. True to form, Mom says to let her know when she's needed and she'll be there with bells on.

One potential crisis down, one more to go—what do I do with *Ningas-Cogon*? My newsmagazine continues to speak truth to the illegitimate regime of Philippines President Ferdinand Marcos, but I've reached a point where I can no longer give it the time and attention it so richly deserves.

I'll need to shut *Ningas-Cogon* down or turn it over to someone who'll continue to oppose Marcos and his criminality as fiercely as my staff and I have. Ultimately, I'm able to pursue that second option courtesy of Alex Esclamado, who runs the *Philippine News* of San Francisco. I sell *Ningas-Cogon* to Esclamado for $1 because I started it to keep an eye on things back home, not to make money.

With my children, Leslie and *Ningas-Cogon* in good hands, I arrive in small town Glynco, Georgia, and dive into the process of understanding how Uncle Sam approaches the enforcement of immigration law. This may sound odd, but I quickly develop a deep bond with Glynco. That's because I'm a coffee drinker, and every single time I enter the government cafeteria, the aroma of coffee brewing in that place is absolutely amazing!

It's not till I'm back in Manhattan that my sudden affinity for the smell of coffee makes sense—Dr. Robert Berke says another baby is on the way!

# 7

# MOGUL MADNESS

**M**y mother loves to talk about the time she took me to see her tarot card reader when I was a teenager, and the mystic couldn't believe the future wealth she saw me enjoying in the future.

"You're going to be very, very rich!" the woman kept repeating in a confident voice. Well, at that nerdy juncture in my life, her prediction was actually a bit of a letdown. I wanted to hear about a fairytale wedding and amazing children, not that I was going to replicate something my father had already accomplished.

Now that I'm 37, married and my second child is on the way, my familial aspirations have largely been realized. But I'm also seeing signs that tarot card reader may have been on to something. Reginald's law firm is generating revenue that would afford our family a comfortable lifestyle even if I were to stop working tomorrow.

Dead set on becoming a One Percenter, my husband is actively looking to acquire and operate a business. In fact, he and one of his brothers, Jean Fugett, purchased a struggling Caribbean radio station, but Reginald quickly discovered why entrepreneurs are seldom absentee owners. Undaunted, my spouse then attempted to buy a meatpacking company and a furniture manufacturing business. He was unsuccessful each time and wound up filing a defamation suit against the furniture company owner that made it possible for Reginald to buy us a wonderful summer home in the Hamptons.

I couldn't be prouder of my beloved's efforts to elevate himself and our family, but I'd be lying if I said I didn't feel occasional tinges of competitiveness. I'm smart, capable, well-educated, and driven just like my husband, and like him, I also want to be an economic pillar for our family. But alas, I feel Reginald is leaving me in the dust.

## IN PURSUIT OF MONEY

So, it's time to step up my wealth-creation game. Marriage is a relationship that calls for lots of baton-passing, but any time high-achieving individuals tie the knot, you can bet there's an area where the baton stays glued to both parties' fingers. Whether it's wages, community and professional acclaim, or even the affection of their children, Type As have a hard time shutting off their competitive instincts. I can vouch for this, having been a valedictorian, cum laude graduate, and student council leader.

Thanks to Uncle Sam, I've got what I need to level the playing field with Reginald, in terms of our efforts to make our family comfortable. The $35,000 lump-sum payment I received from my Immigration and Naturalization Service (INS) settlement should enable me to leave my stamp on the Big Apple's real estate market. After all, I'm the daughter of an entrepreneur, the wife of one, am hard-working and have a terrific grasp of New York State property law, thanks to having recently passed the bar.

As often seems to be the case in my life, it's time for me to start cramming like crazy, and I'm devouring everything I can get my hands on about investing in real estate. I do this as a mom who has one baby on the way, another child who's seven, and a Monday-through-Friday job as a federal immigration attorney. Anyone who's been pregnant can tell you the experience saps your energy and stamina like no other . . . but I can do this.

I cannot, will not, allow Reginald to leave me behind!

My already strong resolve is further solidified by watching Reginald grind through days where he averages five hours of sleep and never complains, even though it's clear to me that he's flirting with burnout. Therefore, after I leave my INS job for the day and Leslie has been fed, read a story, and dispatched to dreamland, I use time that used to go to *Ningas-Cogon* to educate myself about residential real estate.

As sweet Leslie snores, I read, re-read, and re-re-read a captivating book by Roberg G. Allen titled *NOTHING DOWN: A Proven Program That Shows You How to Buy Real Estate With Little Or NO Money Down.* Only after every page and every concept in that book is committed to memory do I start seeking properties for sale. As was the case when I was pregnant with Leslie, my beloved is very solicitous regarding my overall well-being, just as I am with him and his Wall Street law practice and his desire to acquire a business.

I have to smile sometimes, because of all of Manhattan's wannabe power couples, my beloved and I are likely the only African American/ Filipina duo in the mix. But even if we're not, I'd bet a week's salary we're the most fiercely determined to succeed.

Ultimately, I encounter a Filipino couple who are selling just what I'm looking for: a three-story brownstone on Second Avenue and 14th Street in Manhattan. It has a grocery store on the first floor, a tenant on the second floor, and a tenant on the third floor. I buy it for $20,000 in cash, with an eye toward letting the property appreciate for a couple of years before flipping it.

I've been very strategic regarding this purchase, have done scads of research and have made it a point to choose an area where property values are on the upswing. Equally important, the brownstone has extinguished my nagging sense that Reginald is the tide that lifts all Lewis family boats, while I'm just the dutiful wife who goes along for the financial ride.

## EXPANDING OUR FAMILY

But by the time the winter of 1979 appears, my visits to my treasured investment project have tapered off dramatically. Christina Savilla

Nicolas Lewis is supposed to arrive sometime around February 10, 1980, so I want to walk on snow- and ice-covered Manhattan streets as little as possible. My arriving daughter already has a name because Reginald chose Christina Savilla Nicolas, with Savilla being his maternal grandmother's first name. Nicolas is a nod to my family.

I don't think my husband missed a single Lamaze natural childbirth class before I had Leslie in 1973. But six years later, he has a busy corporate law practice to oversee and has missed most of my Lamaze lessons for Christina. That works for me, because having been through childbirth already, I don't need as much hand-holding the second time around. I'm perfectly capable of going through Lamaze and childbirth by myself if that helps my husband keep his eyes on the prize.

I consider myself beyond blessed to have a loving, supportive mother in the Philippines as well as one in the United States. My US mom, Carolyn Fugett, has agreed to make a 200-mile trek from East Baltimore to Manhattan, to assist my husband and me with the expansion of our family. So, Mom has already made her way to Manhattan by February 10th, which is Leslie's seventh birthday. Reginald tells me to stay home and relax, while he goes to a skating rink where Leslie's having a birthday party with classmates.

On February 11, Mom and I travel to Brooklyn to buy a crib for Christina, which will be delivered the next day. That night, as we're finishing dinner in the kitchen of the family brownstone around 9 p.m., I stand up from the table in order to put some dishes in the sink and—Ooooops!

"The baby is coming," I announce in a quiet voice. "My water just broke!"

After checking to see if I'm alright, Reginald hurriedly leaves our brownstone to fetch a car he's rented to whisk everyone to Beth Israel Hospital, the same Manhattan facility where Leslie entered the world. Meanwhile, Mom locates a small luggage bag that's been pre-packed with baby clothes, some articles of clothing for me, and a few small blankets. Everyone has a role to play in Operation Birthing Christina, including Leslie, who gets a brown paper bag that will help me with my

Lamaze breathing. Leslie also gets Mommy a lollipop to keep my mouth from getting parched.

Inside Beth Israel, Reginald sits beside me inside one of the labor rooms, but has forgotten what Lamaze teaches husbands about aiding their partners during childbirth. In fact, at one point, my beloved gets light-headed and nauseous after recalling that I pushed so hard during Leslie's birth that I turned bright red.

At 12:30 a.m. on Tuesday, February 12, 1980, Christina Savilla Nicolas Lewis marks her arrival with a loud, long, healthy bellow. Thank you, Lord! Because her skin and the whites of her eyes are yellowish, Baby Christina has to stay at Beth Israel Hospital a week before she's released to go home. Nothing to worry about because sometimes new-borns have an excessive amount of yellow pigment in their red blood cells.

My new daughter adopts to breastfeeding like a pro, just as Leslie did before her. While Christina is feeding, I've gotten into the habit of staring at her, amazed that we shared the same space for nine months and amazed that God has configured my body to nourish my child now that childbirth is over.

Something else I'm marveling at is how two individuals who have the same parents and who originated in the same womb can end up with such dramatically different personalities. Long before Leslie could walk, it was clear she was demonstrative, demanding, and a natural-born performer. If Christina's early behavior is any indication, she's going to have a calmer, more philosophical approach to life than her sister. I can tell by the way Christina lies in her crib and quietly analyzes her surroundings, including her grandmother, father, and big sister, all of whom couldn't be more thrilled to welcome our newest fam-ily member.

I had prayed Leslie wouldn't feel threatened or resentful about hav-ing to share the spotlight with Christina, following seven years where Leslie had Reginald and me all to herself. Fortunately, she immediately embraces the roles of protector and quasi-mother when it comes to Christina.

I've let the INS know I'm taking several weeks off, thanks to the boatload of vacation and personal time hours I was awarded after winning my lawsuit. I spend a few weeks at our small summer home in Spring Banks, which is located in East Hampton, Long Island.

Focusing exclusively on motherhood, without once allowing immigration law or real estate investing to dominate my thoughts, leads to the most fulfilling time of my life.

While I don't have post-partem depression, I do have a little hormonal episode not long after Christina was born. When she's almost two months old, Reginald, the kids, Reginald's mother, and I all spend Easter weekend in St. Thomas. To facilitate our escape from New York City's cold, we rent a beautiful three-bedroom house where the master bedroom offers a wonderful view of crystalline Cowpet Bay.

After we settle into our place, Leslie's doing what she does best, which is being a gregarious center of attention. This is hard to explain, but for some reason I feel very diminished in this setting, like I don't belong. To be more accurate, I have an acute sense of being unappreciated and taken for granted, which in turn makes me feel jealous of Leslie and Christina, my own daughters! How strange is that?

Feeling "less-than" is not who I am. I've never experienced that sensation before and have never felt it since.

Maybe it's hormonal, or maybe it just isn't my day. Later, I wind up snorkeling in the bay alongside Leslie, who's on a raft. Despite growing up in the Philippines where there's water, water everywhere, I'm a pretty weak swimmer. The deceptively calm water sneakily picks a fight with me when I least expect it . . . now I'm barely above the beautiful turquoise waves . . . now I'm beginning to sink, right in front of my baby! Lord, God, what in the world! This cannot be happening!

But He hasn't forsaken me, because out of nowhere a Good Samaritan on a raft materializes, fishes me out of the water, and accompanies me and Leslie back to shore.

Reginald watches all this from the patio of our rented home and is beyond incensed at Leslie for encouraging me to swim toward her raft in the first place. He had cautioned her not to get on the raft without adult supervision, so she asked if I would join her. And now she's getting an epic tongue lashing from her father, one that I feel is unjustified.

With my hands trembling thanks to all the adrenaline in my system, I'm grateful to be alive. But if I never have another day like this one, that's fine by me.

## BECOMING A REAL ESTATE MOGUL—"LANDED GENTRY, HERE I COME!"

The Lewises are soaring toward a plateau very few families manage to surmount. I see it in little things we're starting to do: our recent impromptu vacation in St. Thomas; the white convertible 450 SL Mercedes sportster Reginald bought himself after we returned; the fact that we've moved upstairs into the triplex section of our five-story Manhattan brownstone and now rent out the first-floor duplex below us.

The days of bouncing checks and scuffling to keep the house phone turned on seem like ancient history. We're enjoying a fairly comfortable lifestyle now; we are still upper-middle class, but are steadily closing in on the next highest socioeconomic category.

My Filipino friends are starting to notice my family's metamorphosis. While they generally steer clear of Reginald, whose temperamental nature and race-consciousness make them uncomfortable, I'm starting to hear praise and even admiration directed toward my soulmate.

Given how unrelenting Reginald is in his pursuit of wealth, it seems it's only a matter of time before the words of my mother's tarot card reader become reality. Reginald's law firm's business-law practice is now a reliable moneymaker, despite naysayers who claimed that opening the first Black firm on Wall Street to focus on corporate law was an arrogant move doomed to fail.

And I'm continuing to do my part with the salary I draw from the INS and with the profits flowing from the brownstone I bought on Second Avenue and 14th Street. The return from my real estate investing makes it possible for me to talk Reginald into partnering with me on another acquisition: a three-building apartment catering to low-income tenants. This newest piece to my fledgling real estate empire costs $175,000, has 32 units, and is located at 10th Avenue between 45th and 46th streets, in the Clinton section of Manhattan.

Not surprisingly, being a wife, raising two young children, working a full-time job, and overseeing two major Manhattan real estate projects has me consistently feeling beat. And the fact that I've never been much of an exercise buff doesn't help.

But the thing is, my spouse and I are only 37. Not 57. We figure that if we work hard up to the age of 50, we've got the rest of our lives to enjoy the financial security we're building. What we're after certainly merits a little fatigue in two people who aren't even 40.

So, I start investigating another potential real estate investment, a 10-story West Side apartment located at 102nd Street and Broadway. My mother and a very good friend who was a classmate at St. Theresa's College, Angie Cruz, and I each chip in $10,000 toward what's known as a purchase-money mortgage. Basically, the owner of property is the mortgager and Mama, Angie, and I will make monthly payments to him, with the goal of eventually owning his building or selling it after it appreciates. If we miss so much as one payment, however, he has the ability to foreclose, and it will be game over for me and my real estate partners.

This transaction couldn't be more pressure-packed. However, as Reginald loves to note, if building wealth were easy, everyone would be doing it. Not to jinx us, but we're making it look pretty easy so far. We have enough money socked away to hold us over for several months in case of an emergency, I have sufficient cash to handle the never-ending maintenance that's a part of owning real estate, and my beloved is putting more disposable income into the stock market.

Life is good, so we may as well double down: I buy another brownstone in a part of northwestern Brooklyn known as Park Slope. From having watched my father, I know you don't get wealthy through doing things by half-measures. So, if I'm not going to go all-in, why bother?

## TRYING TO KEEP UP

One Saturday while Reginald is out growing his business-law practice, at home I've pulled off the rare feat of getting Leslie and Christina to take a nap at the same time. Parents of young children know these are occasions to be savored, because you finally have a moment for yourself! You can use it to sleep, glance at a newspaper, ponder the meaning of life, whatever.

I'm going to use my moment to enjoy a long, relaxing shower. The water has probably been on about 10 minutes when I hear the phone in the master bedroom ringing. So much for 'me time!' I dash out of the shower in my birthday suit, leaving behind wet footprints in my haste to keep the phone from waking up the kids.

Some persistent guy on the phone tries to convince me to let him come by and pitch the latest Encyclopedia Britannica. Awesome. I'm soaking wet, freezing, can hear Christina stirring from her nap, and this gentleman wants to talk about encyclopedias.

I feel chills after returning to the bathroom and even sneeze a couple of times, but think nothing of it. But during the weekend the sneezing becomes coughing, and by Monday I'm hacking so much that I call in sick rather than expose everyone in the office to whatever it is that I have.

Instead of getting better, the coughing progresses to the point where my back hurts every time I cough. A dear friend who attended the University of the Philippines with me, Suzette Bagaybagayan Rutherford, calls and hears my coughing.

"Loida, what's that?" Suzette wants to know.

"I have a little head cold," I tell her. "Every time I cough, though, it pains my back."

"Loida, that sounds serious. Go get an X-ray!"

I take Suzette's advice and after taking an X-ray, the physician I visit prescribes antibiotics for tuberculosis. It's a disease I had as a six-year-old, which the X-ray bears mute testimony to when my doctor shows me a scar on one of my lungs.

I'm pretty sure I know why I'm having this second encounter with TB. For one thing, in my position with the INS I'm constantly in contact with immigrants from countries that have lower health standards than the United States'. Second, I'm simply doing too many things. I'm overburdened, which I have no doubt has weakened my immune system.

I've got the will and the work ethic to emulate my husband's brutal, workaholic lifestyle, but it may be that my body won't allow me to run nonstop like he does. To find out, I get plenty of rest at home and drink lots of liquids, which helps the coughing to subside.

Hoping my TB is waving the white flag, I end my sick leave and head back to my INS job. And after a day or two back in the office, the coughing returns with a vengeance.

So, this time I burn another week of sick leave and just stay home, which I'd prefer not to do. Because although I need to rest, I also don't want to make my family ill. Thankfully, my cough goes away again and I head back to the INS. And as soon as I return, the coughing starts back up again.

My body clearly isn't built to handle the routine I'm subjecting it to. I gave it my best shot, but something has to fall off my itinerary. As much as it pains me to admit it, I think my real estate business needs to go by the wayside.

With tremendous reluctance and sadness, I shut down my Superwoman audition. For three months I stay at home, getting myself 100% well as I take care of my darling girls, one of whom isn't 1 yet. While I'm on extended sick leave from the INS, I sell my Brooklyn brownstone. I have no qualms about taking this step because my well-being is infinitely more important than having ownership of material things.

## Real Estate with a Conscience

After I get my health back, unusually harsh winter weather puts my core beliefs to the test: Do I make my monthly mortgage payment on the 10-story West Side apartment I bought with Mama and my friend Angie Cruz, or do I instead buy heating oil for the tenants, so they can remain warm? I don't need to mull this one over for a second—NO ONE is freezing in a dwelling I'm associated with. We will not be responsible for even one case of frostbite, and Mama and Angie concur.

So, as soon as I convert my monthly mortgage payment into heating oil, like clockwork the apartment owner sues us for foreclosure, which he's able to do under the terms of our contract. For some people, legal correctness and moral correctness have nothing to do with one another.

My beloved advises that filing bankruptcy will stop the landlord in his tracks, so we hire an attorney and pay him $10,000 up front to have 102nd Realty Company, a limited liability chapter S corporation I created, file Chapter 11 in US Bankruptcy Court.

Reginald assumes oversight of the 32-unit apartment building we bought together for $175,000 on 10th Avenue, between 45th and 46th streets. Regarding the very first property that I purchased, the three-story brownstone on 2nd Avenue and 14th Street that cost $20,000, I sell it after two years for three times what I paid for it.

I've thought an awful lot about my foray into New York City's real estate market. It's taught me a lot about myself and my place in the world. First and foremost, what's the point of owning half the real estate in Manhattan if you can't do so in good health?

There is no point. So, I've elevated raising my children and safeguarding my health over creating wealth. I'm not cut out for it physically or mentally, because if presented with a choice between keeping scores of people from freezing or making a business payment, people will win every single time.

Second, it's time for me to dial back on my lifelong habit of trying to do a thousand things simultaneously. My real estate adventure made it real clear that it's time to stop spreading myself too thin. Also, being a good mother, wife, and federal immigration attorney gives me more than enough to concentrate on.

So, no more empire-building for me. In retrospect, my efforts to become a real estate mogul were, as my beloved is wont to say, "half-assed."

Will the amazing wealth that Mama's tarot card reader foresaw for me still come to pass? We shall see.

# 8

# "YOU REPRESENT ME!"

I'm teaching my daughters Leslie and Christina to adhere to the Golden Rule, to respect their elders, to have open minds and compassionate hearts, and to comport themselves with postures befitting royalty.

But now that they're 10 and 3, respectively, it's clear they need something I'll never be able to give them, and that's a roadmap for navigating America as Black females. It pains me to admit this, but I'm seeing that Reginald's take on America's discriminatory treatment of non-White citizens is on-point.

I get a graphic demonstration of this while visiting Leslie's predominantly White, private school for girls on the Upper East Side of Manhattan. Her sixth-grade teacher is wonderfully patient and encouraging when White kids answer questions in class, but impatient and dismissive when students of color have their turn.

Along with their long, shiny black curls, my offspring have beautiful bronze skin that means they'll always be categorized as Black Americans. To realize their full potential, African American children need parents who are fierce advocates, plus they need confidence-building support systems.

After looking everywhere, I think I've found a desperately needed Afrocentric ally, within the pages of the *New York Times*, no less. I'm referring to an article about the Jack and Jill of America organization, which was created by African American mothers in 1938 to stimulate their children's social and cultural development.

I immediately pick up my kitchen phone and dial the operator to get a New York City telephone number for Jack and Jill. An accommodating lady named Ardith Hill answers and, without once making note of my thick Philippines accent, walks me through Jack and Jill's mission of supporting middle-class African American children.

I want Leslie and Christina to be around Black children who go on skiing trips to Colorado, take Caribbean vacations during the winter, and attend private schools where they're often the only Black student in their class. This is something Reginald and I agree on.

Before getting off the phone with Ardith, I commit to buying tickets to a Jack and Jill fundraising event. I know Jack and Jill gets criticized in some Black circles for being elitist, but Ardith is totally unapologetic about Jack and Jill's mandate.

"This is an organization for African American children," she says. "Your girls are African Americans."

I think this may be her offhanded way of letting me know some of the moms may have problems with my Asian background. Sure enough, a few vote against admitting me, but when all the votes are tallied, I make it into Jack and Jill easily, so Leslie and Christina are in!

I volunteer to hold a Jack and Jill shindig in my brownstone for a group of roughly 20 kids and their mothers. The event winds up being the talk of the town because I pull out all the stops and even hire a magician. I'm told one Jack and Jill mother was highly critical of my gathering, likely because I went above and beyond the norm. The important thing is that Leslie, Christina, and the other children have a blast, as do most of their mothers.

My girls and I come to look forward to Jack and Jill activities, which include attending Broadway shows, going to museums, and holding birthday parties. My girls and I develop lifelong friendships as a result of our association with Jack and Jill.

The organization's name comes up often when we have dinner on the third floor of our brownstone, and Reginald asks Leslie and Christina how their days went. Afterward, Reginald will trundle back upstairs to the fifth floor of our brownstone, back into his penthouse lair, where he ponders how to acquire a sizeable business that's already profitable.

His fifth-floor study has an ample skylight, a vintage wooden French farmer's desk, a blue velour couch that's great for short naps, and Reginald's precious Bose stereo system. Whenever I go upstairs to check on him, he's usually in the middle of an animated business conversation on his desk phone or reading up on companies that might make potential acquisition targets.

His bruising failure to seize his third acquisition target—a leisure furniture company in California—after working on the project for 18 arduous months has made Reginald even more determined to execute a corporate takeover. Seated behind his desk, surrounded by cigar smoke as Barry White quietly croons in the background, Reginald is convinced he's on the verge of a trailblazing business acquisition.

"The fourth time will be a charm," he tells me laughingly. "This isn't a sprint; it's a *marathon*." I smile upon hearing these words because I know full well that Reginald won't quit till he gets the job done.

The other reason I smile is because my beloved currently has a huge fish on the line, one that will result in a headline-generating deal worth roughly $22 million. Reginald talks freely about his ongoing acquisition attempt, which is jangling his nerves and making him more brusque and short-tempered than usual.

My take on all this is, do it! Go for it! I've already tried to operate in mogul mode and found my body isn't built for it. One of the most empowering things you can accomplish in life is accurately mapping your strengths and weaknesses and determining what makes you happy.

Along those lines, I haven't been deriving a lot of joy lately from my employer, the Immigration and Naturalization Service (INS). They must have an ax to grind where I'm concerned.

I thought that after I successfully sued them for discrimination and wound up winning three years of back pay and several months of vacation and personal time, they'd understand that I will always fight for fairness and justice. I was wrong.

For some reason, they've decided not to promote me from grade level GS-11 to GS-12, a pro forma move that's based more on service time than anything. In addition to having been around long enough to merit a GS-12 ranking, my performance as an immigration trial attorney has consistently been exemplary.

I wind up filing another discrimination lawsuit against my employer and introduce into evidence a handwritten note from the INS bureaucrat in Washington, D.C., who oversees my division: "What has Loida done to deserve getting promoted?"

Included in my complaint is a list of cases I've handled that were referred to me by the receptionist, underscoring the fact that no other general attorney responds to queries the receptionist receives over the telephone and in-person. I also add in my complaint that the INS is retaliating against me because I won my previous discrimination case.

I guess the INS decides that fighting me again doesn't make any sense. Without going through another hearing before an administrative judge, the agency simply promotes me and awards me $5,000 in deferred salary to cover what I lost by not getting promoted 18 months earlier.

I wind up giving Reginald the $5,000 to thank him for his financial, legal, and emotional support when tuberculosis was torching my dreams of mastering New York City's real estate scene.

"Wow, Babe, thank you!" he says with a belly laugh as he studies my check. "When are you suing those federal sons of bitches again?"

Hopefully never, Reginald. Hopefully never.

## GETTING INTO A FASHIONABLE INDUSTRY

Today, January 29, 1984, Reginald Francis Lewis bought the McCall Pattern Company, which designs, manufactures, and markets home sewing patterns. The nation's financial press is agog over Reginald's groundbreaking $22.5-million buyout.

For me, as well as for my beloved, the transaction is incredibly exciting and exhilarating. Having been privy to all the dreaming, preparation, hard work, and failure that preceded McCall, I am grateful to God and am thankful for my soulmate's tenacity and moxie.

I knew Reginald was going to be successful and am quietly observing him to see if fame and fortune are changing him in subtle, and not so subtle, ways. What I'm seeing thus far is that he's the exact same person when it comes to interacting with strangers, friends, relatives, and Leslie, Christina, and me. He's totally free of pretension or airs.

Whatever qualities someone loved or disliked about Reginald prior to the McCall buyout, I think they'll find them in equal measure post-McCall.

Leslie and Christina are both aware Daddy has done something that's momentous and beyond the ken of most businesspeople, Black or White. While Christina, who's a few days from turning 4, doesn't fully grasp the import of her dad's McCall Pattern acquisition, Leslie clearly does at nearly 11. I let them both know they have every right to be proud of their father, but that his accomplishments don't make them the least bit special or exalted.

A few weeks into the McCall acquisition, Reginald reminds me on at least two occasions that, "You represent me!" He doesn't elaborate further, but I'm sure this is a veiled reference to the frumpiness quotient of my clothing choices.

It's a fairly high quotient, admittedly, but I dress with an eye toward utility, not fashion. On the other hand, my beloved envisions me dressing with the eye-catching style of Jackie Kennedy. This didn't start with McCall—following Leslie's birth, he gave me a Mikimoto pearl necklace from Bergdorf Goodman, a Fifth Avenue luxury department store, to wear during Leslie's baptism on July 4, 1973.

This is crazy, but with my practical nature I felt the necklace was way too expensive, so I returned it. Sounding as if his feelings were slightly bruised, Reginald told me, "Well, Loida, it's a gift to you. It's yours, so you can do whatever you want."

I think he was disappointed to find his woman didn't have class and was basically a hick-town girl from a small Philippines province.

Those pearls cost so much that I was able to exchange them for five pieces of clothing, including a suede skirt, after I took them back to Bergdorf Goodman. I just felt I needed nice work clothes more than a Mikimoto necklace, even though it looked exquisite on me the one time I wore it.

A lot of time passed before my beloved gave me serious jewelry again. But it was worth the wait, in light of receiving a Tiffany diamond necklace and earrings when I turned 40, a four-carat diamond ring on our twentieth anniversary, and a ruby necklace and earrings for my 45th birthday. I learned my lesson—I'm not stupid!

## QUIETLY LEARNING THE BUSINESS

My man has purchased the McCall Pattern Company. . . . I quietly repeat that to myself when things get a little too surreal. Especially in light of the fact that he used a leveraged-buyout deal structure where he didn't put a cent of his money into the transaction. As thrilled as I am for Reginald, I'm equally happy for myself, because if the McCall Pattern deal had cratered, he would have been a very, very difficult person to live with. In addition, we would have had to sell our summer home in East Hampton to pay legal, accounting, and other fees generated by a failed business deal. Failure was definitely not an option this time around.

I vividly recall how my husband reacted after his failed attempts to buy Parks Sausage, the California furniture manufacturer, and a group of six radio stations. Few people know that as hard as Reginald can be on others, he's about 10 times harder on himself.

And when he falls short of his lofty expectations, like failing to close three consecutive major business deals, the brooding, cussing, and self-doubt that results verges on being unbearable. Reginald tries to execute business transactions totally free of emotion, but he's too passionate to pull that off, precipitating an emotional firestorm when he fails.

But that always dies down and is followed by a period where he dispassionately analyzes his moves and how they may have worked against him. After much soul-searching and reflection on his three unsuccessful attempts to buy corporations, he came up with a three-word explanation for not crossing the finish line: "I wasn't ready."

With that in mind, he religiously studied successful leveraged buy-out (LBO) acquisitions executed by the 1980s top LBO specialists: Henry Kravis, Sir Jimmy Goldsmith, Ronald Perelman, and Ted Forstmann.

That enabled my husband to finally figure out what he was doing wrong—he was wearing too many hats. Reginald was acting as his own accountant, legal advisor, and investment banker instead of hiring experts to represent him in those areas.

So, for the McCall Pattern Company transaction, he retains the services of investment banker Phyllis Schless, of Bear, Stearns & Co., seasoned business attorney Tom Lamia, and makes Price Waterhouse his accounting firm.

Regarding his three abortive attempts to buy businesses prior to McCall, Reginald has a nagging suspicious that in each case, even with Black-owned Parks Sausages, the sellers may have doubted that a young Black man was capable of consummating a multimillion-dollar acquisition.

So for McCall, I agree with his decision to resort to subterfuge and make it appear he represents an investment group. When the time comes to close the transaction, Reginald reveals he's actually going to be the majority owner.

I take no credit for the McCall Pattern Company acquisition but am tickled to death the stars have finally aligned.

Now that Reginald owns the corporation, he begins showing up at McCall's Manhattan headquarters on Park Avenue to let McCall's leaders know of his plans for the 114-year-old business.

Reginald has largely turned his back on his law firm at 99 Wall Street, which is now called Lewis and Clarkson to reflect the presence of Charles Clarkson, a White lawyer Reginald hired following Charles' graduation from Brooklyn Law School.

My husband's main sparring partner within McCall is the chief executive officer (CEO), Earle Angstadt, who's 17 years Reginald's senior and has been with McCall for 14 years. In light of the gaps in their ages and his sewing-pattern experience, Earle probably thought he'd be a mentor to my husband.

I thought the dynamic might play out that way too, so during Reginald's first week of ownership, I'm amazed at how often he's on our brownstone telephone, loudly and profanely telling Earle there's a new sheriff in town and things are going to be done differently. Earle's receiving a critical first test from McCall's new owner, and if Earle doesn't stand up for himself and immediately show some backbone, my husband will have zero respect for McCall's CEO.

I don't agree with Reginald's methodology, but I understand what's going on, having watched him fight and hustle for 14 years to become the owner of an ongoing business. Now that he's finally made it, Reginald has no intention of failing and wants managers who are as eager to run through brick walls as he is.

By Reginald's second week of ownership, Earle has had enough and growls back at Reginald, "Don't you ever talk to me that way!" Earle has unwittingly done the right thing, because Reginald tends to steam-roller people with weak personalities.

I know about this back and forth because Reginald excitedly fills me in every night regarding what's going on with McCall, and how imperative it is that he immediately rein in Earle and his second in command, Chief Operating Officer Bob Hermann.

Reginald consistently makes me shake my head. I've never met anyone with his moxie, not even my businessman father. I love Reginald unconditionally and with all my heart and admire him more than anyone on earth. He's a man with immense gifts, but he's not perfect. No one is.

Now that McCall Pattern is finally within his grasp, I'm amazed how unemotionally Reginald regards his company. He speaks incessantly of having two ironclad McCall Pattern Company goals: making it more profitable than it's ever been in more than a century of existence and using it as a wealth-generating vehicle.

Period.

The second part of that equation is partially linked to management, so Reginald's paying himself a generous salary that's comparable to what most CEOs running multimillion-dollar corporations earn. The bump in our family income means we no longer need a tenant in our brownstone's first-floor duplex. Reginald's turned that space into an informal art gallery full of pieces by Romare Bearden and other renowned artists whose works my spouse is starting to collect.

Our summer home in the Hamptons is paid off, we have plenty of cash saved, and Reginald recently bought a big, blue Mercedes sedan to go with the little, white Mercedes sportster we already had. Reginald loves nothing more than surprising his relatives in Baltimore with expensive gifts, and his mother and I receive expensive clothing and jewelry when we least expect it.

This is made possible by McCall's profitability, which I'm learning is the focus of the high-decibel conversations Reginald constantly has with Earle Angstadt and Bob Hermann.

Long before Reginald entered the sewing-pattern arena, McCall and its main competitors, Butterick and Vogue, had a habit of periodically launching price wars to undercut the competition. After initially heeding Angstadt's advice to lower the price of McCall's patterns, and then losing money, my husband went contrarian. He raised the price of McCall's sewing patterns the next time a price war was waged.

This undergirded a large jump in net sales and a small decrease in market share, increasing McCall's profitability. I have no idea where Reginald, a business attorney by training, got the idea to execute this strategy, which sewing-pattern industry executives were oblivious to.

Thanks to osmosis, I'm gradually becoming a sewing-pattern expert myself. This is because my beloved constantly talks to me about McCall, sometimes simply to have a sympathetic ear, sometimes to take my temperature on a business initiative he's considering.

This is ironic because I can't sew a lick, would have difficulty turning on a sewing machine, and have never been mistaken for a clotheshorse. But I do have a good grasp of business principles, thanks to my father and mother. And that grasp is being continually honed by my husband, although I can't take a deep dive into McCall and its operations like Reginald does.

The time demands of caring for Leslie and Christina and of working as a federal attorney wouldn't allow for that.

I'm perfectly content observing from afar and serving as a McCall touchstone whenever Reginald needs one. I watch with fascination as he comes up with money-making innovations such as using idle sewing-pattern presses to print greeting cards. And I applaud his decision to spruce up McCall's dowdy image by having actresses Diahann Carroll and Brooke Shields photographed wearing McCall clothing.

Not to come off as a doting, starstruck wife, I'm stunned my husband is showing an industry that's been around for more than a century improved ways to do business. This time last year he didn't know anything about the sewing-pattern landscape, its main players, market trends, etc. His ability to quickly wrap his brain around tremendously complex fact patterns and then master them is astounding. Sure, that's what attorneys do, but now we're talking about doing it as the first-time owner of a multimillion-dollar business.

Effortlessly gliding from strength to strength, McCall's chairman launches a succession of brilliant financial stratagems designed to extract maximum value from the McCall Pattern Company, beginning with a sale-leaseback arrangement involving the sale of a McCall facility in Kansas to a company Reginald created. The move puts $5.5 million on McCall's balance sheet and generates a commitment for McCall to pay my beloved $1,152,000 annually over a 10-year period.

Thanks to my curious nature, and the fact that I listen carefully when my husband discusses McCall, my knowledge of things such as "public equity markets," "shareholder return," and "subordinated debentures" is growing by leaps and bounds. I'm starting to develop a view-from-40,000-feet perspective of corporations that business owners need to survive.

But aside from Reginald and me, no one else is aware of my quiet transformation. I'm largely seen as Reginald's wife, or Leslie and Christina's mom, which is how things should be. I'm delighted to be defined as the wife and mother in the Lewis family but would be even happier if I were 100% anonymous.

## THANKING GOD FOR OUR BLESSINGS

In the fall of 1986, Reginald starts entertaining the possibility of selling McCall, just cashing in his chips and walking away. Music to my ears! Serving as McCall's owner and chairman has been terrifically enjoyable for my husband, but at the same time, the experience has undeniably been grueling.

He'd never cast it in these terms, but it's been a grind that's greedily devoured my man's focus, energy, and time. I tell him as much when he asks what I think of selling McCall. So, when my spouse divests McCall to the British-based John Crowther Group for $65 million in June 1987, I'm over the moon. I'm not going to lie!

His imagination and hard-driving nature catapulted McCall to its two most profitable years ever, resulting in tens of millions of dollars flowing into Reginald's bank account.

At 44, Reginald says he's more than ready to decompress and simply enjoy life with his three beautiful Lewis ladies, after spending the bulk of his life kicking open doors and then working like a man possessed.

Words can't describe how proud I am of Reginald.

The night the McCall sale is finalized, I go to Mass to thank God for the embarrassment of riches—literal and figurative—He's bestowed upon my family. And I make it a point to thank Him for the biggest blessing of all, which is the fact that Leslie and Christina are growing up with good heads on their shoulders and with their hearts in the right place.

"Father God, whatever the future holds for the Lewis family, I pray that You'll always keep my girls centered and well-adjusted.

Amen."

# 9

# THE LIFE OF RILEY

I thought Reginald was exiting the corporate takeover game after selling the McCall Pattern Company. But there's been a change of plans, a gargantuan one I'm working to wrap my brain around.

The same month Reginald sells McCall, June 1987, he positions himself to go after Beatrice International Foods, a Chicago-based multinational with 64 operating units in 31 countries. To put this undertaking in perspective, my husband is trying to accomplish the largest offshore leveraged buyout ever attempted!

Working in tandem with his best friend Cleveland "Cleve" Christophe, a former Citibank exec who'd overseen the organization's operations in Colombia, Jamaica, and France before retiring, my beloved has submitted a $985 million offer for Beatrice International.

Whenever corporate takeover titans lasso multibillion-dollar firms, they're typically assisted by legions of accountants, lawyers, and other advisors. Reginald is looking to replicate all that manpower with just two people, himself and Cleve. Okay, I finally get it—I'm married to someone whose ambition knows no bounds.

Moving forward, if Reginald Francis Lewis says he wants to buy Macy's or Boeing or IBM, I won't even bat an eye. I'll simply ask what, if anything, I can do to aid him, just as I did a few days ago when he told me about Beatrice International Foods.

The most helpful thing I can do right now, my spouse tells me, is to head to the South of France with the girls. That's where Reginald has arranged for us to vacation for the summer, his gift to the family following McCall.

So, Leslie, Christina, and I jet off to Côte d'Azur on the French Riviera, while Reginald stays behind in Manhattan to vie for Beatrice International Foods along with Cleve. My beloved will then join his family in France about a week later than planned.

With my daughters in tow, I make my way to the enclave of Castellaras le Vieux, which is full of ritzy villas and overlooks the Mediterranean. We're spending the bulk of August 1987 in a four-bedroom villa that's one of 80 charming units situated on a hill directly beside the ocean.

The enclave of Castellaras le Vieux contains a fourteenth-century chapel, several tennis courts, and two swimming pools. The villa we're renting has a terrace offering superb views of old olive trees, brilliant lavender-colored bougainvilleas, and other well-manicured summer flowers that look like they were transplanted from Manhattan's ubiquitous sidewalk flower stands.

If the three of us have any remaining doubts about our new station in life, they're permanently erased after the girls and I retain the services of a private chef and a housekeeper. I can't speak for Leslie and Christina, but after 10 minutes of pampering inside our ultra-exclusive South of France villa, I'm ready for a lot more.

Taking into account our picturesque locale, French food that's cooked to perfection in our villa, wonderful weather, and friendly European and US tourists, what's not to like? This is clearly going to be an August to remember.

As we wait for Reginald to join us, I take the girls on day trips to nearby Mougins, a charming Medieval village where Picasso lived.

We also visit Cannes, the site of the world-renowned film festival, and Grasse, a French Riviera town that's central to France's perfume industry.

Away from the hustle and bustle of Manhattan, my mind untethered from the Immigration and Naturalization Service (INS), McCall, and the mess Ferdinand Marcos has made of Philippine government, I've never felt so thoroughly relaxed.

We have to be back in Manhattan by September so my daughters can start school, but if that weren't the case, I'd have no problem spending August and September in Cote d'Azur. Every night after the girls fall asleep, my thoughts drift to Reginald. How is Beatrice International Foods coming along, and is he eating properly and getting enough rest?

When my beloved finally arrives, he's beyond euphoric over the Beatrice International Foods deal, which I'm pleased to discover is having an aphrodisiac effect on him. Like it did with me, Castellaras le Vieux quickly melts away the tensions and stresses Reginald has accumulated over the years.

Even the girls seem uncharacteristically carefree and relaxed, leading me to wonder if my husband and I are putting too much pressure on them to succeed academically and be model citizens. I make a mental note to address this when we get back home, because life is hard enough without feeling you can never make a misstep because it might reflect unfavorably on your family's legacy.

Right now, Leslie and Christina are two happy-go-lucky girls delighted to be vacationing in the South of France with their parents. Still, I'm feeling a need to protect them from their father's fast-growing notoriety. At the moment, though, the main thing my girls need is protection from their father's funny bone.

He's in rare form in Castellaras le Vieux, smiling broadly and cracking jokes like they're going out of style. Reginald has teamed up with his primary straight woman, Leslie, who he's egging on to tell one of his favorite jokes.

I couldn't repeat the setup if my life depended on it, but the joke's punchline has to do with a poor pig that winds up with three legs. Reginald keeps prodding Leslie, who's very much a ham (pun intended), to act out the joke. And each time she does, Reginald howls and howls as if hearing it for the first time.

This is great! It's so incredibly rare for us to share long stretches of uninterrupted quality time.

Reginald occasionally steals away for long-distance calls with business advisors. But those conversations are seldom lengthy, and when Reginald returns, we get his undivided attention every single time.

It's fairly rare for the Lewis women to have Reginald to ourselves. Most of his time is devoured by work, so he makes it a point to always be in the moment when with Leslie and Christina. However, when it's just him and me, I'm his reliable business sounding board. So, he typically talks to me about what he's working on, and I'm an active listener.

The amazing job he did putting together the financing for the McCall Pattern Company, and the skillful way he operated the firm, earned him a very influential fan: financier Michael Milken, who oversees the high-yield bond department of investment bank Drexel, Burnham, Lambert.

The man at the center of the leveraged buyout craze utilized by corporate raiders during the 1980s, Michael has gotten Drexel to pledge $1 billion in backing for Reginald to acquire Beatrice International Foods.

As soon as Reginald and Cleve can close the deal, they plan to sell all of Beatrice International Foods' operating units, except for those located in Western Europe. This will enable them to avoid being saddled with debt payments on $1 billion, a strategy that's brilliant in its audacity as well as its simplicity.

When the media finally catches on to what Reginald is doing with Beatrice International Foods, all hell breaks loose. I'm not sure how, but a few enterprising journalists manage to contact us at Castellaras le Vieux, including someone working for *Time* magazine. Reginald cuts that interview short because the reporter wants to focus primarily on my spouse's race instead of on the groundbreaking things Reginald's doing as a businessman.

But Reginald's irritation quickly blows over because it's difficult for anything to get you down when you're relaxing in the South of France.

After August 1987 draws to a close, we return to Manhattan. Not long afterward, Reginald and Cleve are flying around the globe in chartered jets to personally inspect Beatrice International Foods' operating units.

Meanwhile, I'm back at the INS. Since returning to Manhattan, my mind often wanders back to Castellaras le Vieux because I'm keen on visiting France again at the earliest opportunity.

As the old saying goes, be careful what you wish for.

## LEAVING THE INS

What do say after your spouse purchases a $1-billion-dollar, multinational corporation, in a deal that had naysayers making him the poster boy for hubris run amok?

I don't know the answer to that. So, I simply hug Reginald Lewis, the new chairman of TLC Beatrice International Holdings, Inc., so forcefully inside our Manhattan brownstone that I squeeze the breath out of him. No one knows Reginald's Alice-in-Wonderland journey better than the two of us.

It's the morning of Wednesday, December 2, 1987, the day after Reginald barely met a midnight deadline to close on Beatrice International Foods. A billion-dollar deal he only put $15 million of his money into to acquire 51% of the behemoth company.

The kids are already in school, and I'm about to dash off to the INS office, while my beloved is going to Lewis & Clarkson at 99 Wall Street. His stylish Italian suit fits him so nicely that Reginald receives an approving once-over from his wife.

"I'm quitting INS this week," I inform Reginald, grinning widely even though I'm quite serious. "Turning in my resignation today."

"What's taken so long? You should have been outta there."

"Now you tell me!"

"Let's hit the Hamptons Saturday," Reginald says, moving toward the stairwell. "There's something out there you might find interesting. . . . "

On Saturday, my family piles into our big Mercedes sedan, and Reginald starts driving toward Long Island. He refuses to say where we're going or what he's so excited about, so I sit back and enjoy the two-hour ride.

Getting a kick out of being mysterious, my spouse exits Montauk Highway and turns on to a narrow, mile-and-a-half-long asphalt lane that wends through pastoral meadows and forests. A monstrously large Georgian mansion soon begins to loom in the distance. Seriously puzzled, I turn to Reginald.

"Whose house is this?"

"This is Broadview. In Amangansett, Long Island. Maybe it's our house!" This is followed by a booming laugh. "Let's find out."

Pivoting on the front passenger seat of our car, I turn and look at Reginald, to see if he's serious. Naturally, he is. You'd think I'd have learned by now not to be surprised by anything this man says or does.

A realtor is cooling her heels inside a Jaguar parked in front of Broadview, which has 25 rooms and is on five and a half majestic acres of land, near a 75-foot high bluff overlooking the deep blue waters of the Atlantic Ocean and Gardiners Bay. Gawking at Broadview, feeling downright Lilliputian in its presence, I scrunch up my face—this place is waaaaaay too big for four people.

We're ushered inside the newly renovated mansion, which boasts a double-size living room, a double-size dining room with two dining tables that each seat 12, a double-size master bedroom with separate his and hers dressing rooms. Broadview's other luxurious touches include a large TV room next to a billiard room, what looks to be an Olympic outdoor swimming pool, and an enclosed garden room that easily has 100 window panes.

*Susmariosep*!!!

While Broadview is intimidating me, the girls are loving it. And judging from the smitten look on Reginald's face, he's already head over heels. No question that this 25-room mansion represents a dramatic upgrade over the three-bedroom vacation house we've grown used to visiting in East Hampton.

Being the lone dissenting vote in a family of four never works out, so Reginald and the girls prevail when he buys Broadview, after whittling the price down to $3.6 million, from $4 million.

Rosemary Sheehan, who was the seller's consultant, helps me find a housekeeper, Jamaica-born Rena Hewie, and we hire Dalma Walker to be Broadview's chef.

Because it's such a long trek from the kitchen to the dining room, Rena recommends that her boyfriend, Lucien Stoutt, an immigrant from the Caribbean island of Tortola, work as our butler.

From buying Beatrice International Foods, to vacationing in Castellaras le Vieux, to snapping up Broadview, there's no question my family and I are bona fide One Percenters now.

Before I have an opportunity to fully understand this transition, and how I can leverage my new socioeconomic status to affect causes that are important to me, my family and I go through our biggest change yet.

## LEAVING NEW YORK

When Reginald was a boy growing up in Baltimore, he loved hearing the tales his maternal grandfather, Sam Cooper, told about Paris. Mr. Cooper spoke of the City of Light in almost mythical terms, especially when it came to the warm reception Parisians gave him during World War I, when he was a G.I. stationed in Europe.

Mr. Cooper spoke with bitterness of his subsequent return to Baltimore, and how White Americans refused to accord him the same respect he received every day on the boulevards of Paris. For African Americans like Mr. Cooper, returning to the United States from World War I meant sliding back into second-class citizenship.

So, Paris has always been a magical place for my beloved. He and his grandfather may be separated by age, but I view them as virtual twins: Both are highly intelligent, terrifically hot-tempered, perceptive, and unwilling to put up with any race-based crap.

Mr. Cooper's influence explains why my husband is fascinated by all things French and why he took the trouble to become reasonably fluent in the language.

Now that he's sold off the Canadian, South American, and Australian components of TLC Beatrice to pay down debt, and left the European components intact, Reginald informs me of his desire to operate out of Paris. I don't have a problem with that. No one in our family does.

So, Reginald, the girls, and I move to Paris in the summer of 1988, into a dwelling that would put a huge grin on Mr. Cooper's face if he were alive to see it.

Leslie and Christina are immediately enrolled in the École Active Bilange Jeannine Manuel international school, in the tenth grade and the third grade, respectively. With the exception of English literature, all of their instruction is in French.

By December, both of my daughters are conversing pretty decently in French. Reginald takes an immersive French language course in the South of France, whereas I enroll in a French class offered by the British Institute, a block from our new home.

Our place is undergoing renovation when we first arrive, so we stay at the luxury Hotel de Crillon, where our room overlooks the Place de la Concorde, a major public square with eighteenth-century Rococo style fountains and an Egyptian obelisk.

After the interior of our apartment has been totally refurbished, we move into a 25-room unit that's on the second floor of a five-story building directly behind the Assemblée Nationale, the equivalent of the US Congress.

Reginald worked like a dog to attain wealth and has no problem enjoying every perk that comes with his new status. Therefore, we have separate chauffeurs to squire us around Paris. Reginald's driver, Patrick Lelong, transports his boss inside a top-of-the-line, black Mercedes limo, while my chauffeur, Raymond Peuchaud, takes me where I need to go in a Renault.

To round out the transportation side of things, Reginald has TLC Beatrice buy a high-end Bombardier Challenger corporate jet that's capable of crossing the Atlantic Ocean. Reginald says the Challenger is a godsend when he needs to check on TLC Beatrice's operations, which are primarily concentrated in Western Europe now.

In a typical day he'll travel to corporate units in Italy, Spain, and Brussels, before returning to our apartment at 9 Place du Palais Bourbon in the city's 7th district, easily the most exclusive slice of Paris. Upon entering our two-story home, which is on the west bank of the River Seine, you encounter a huge foyer that's the size of a studio apartment and immediately see a spacious dining room straight ahead that has an entryway to a garden that's situated atop our ground-floor garage. The kitchen has a stairwell that descends to a floor containing a bedroom for our oldest daughter, Leslie, as well as a guestroom.

Back upstairs, to the left of the foyer is a double living room. The first cavernous room is dominated by a brown baby grand piano and eighteenth-century furniture. The adjoining space contains a massive French eighteenth-century desk and another living room that's full of French furniture. This serves as Reg's study.

Turn left after leaving the study and you'll encounter the master bedroom. Next to that is a study where I have reinvented myself as an author of books teaching immigrants how to get into the United States. Not far from my study is Christina's bedroom, then a bathroom at the end of the hallway.

Upon exiting our building, we're within walking distance of three world-renowned museums, a Paris metro station, and are roughly a mile from the Eiffel Tower.

Parisians are a pretty unflappable lot, but even their ears perk up and eyebrows levitate when I tell them I reside in the 7th district, or the 7th *arrondissement* as the French call it. I try to avoid discussing where I live because I find it embarrassing when people make a fuss over it.

Reg, on the other hand, loves it. He acts as if nothing could be more natural than hanging out where France's uber elite have gravitated since the seventeenth century. Parisians are invariably stunned when they learn Reg owns the two huge companies that have a stranglehold on Paris' supermarket business, Leader Price and Franprix.

Like their father, Leslie and Christina have morphed into card-carrying members of the French bourgeois with laudable ease.

Prior to setting off for Harvard, Leslie navigates Paris like a native. Leslie's akin to Reg in that at times she can be terrifically intense. Blunt. Demonstrative. And they're both able to fill a room with incandescent charm and sparkling personality, seemingly at will.

Christina is more artsy and introspective, has my sensitive, intuitive nature, is analytical like her father, and is probably the most proficient French speaker of the family. Christina enjoys Paris and its cultural offerings but always seems to approach the city with a bit of detachment.

Me, I've had no problems adjusting to our new 7th district existence. Who couldn't get accustomed to the very best life has to offer, served up against a backdrop of the world's most cosmopolitan city?

Regarding our new home, the owner of our apartment building lent us the brown walnut concert piano that graces our living room. Given that most folks don't have baby grands in their homes, I'm adamant about the girls learning to play the piano. Before she headed off to Harvard, Leslie wasn't terribly interested in piano lessons, although she grudgingly learned to play Scott Joplin's "The Entertainer."

But Christina takes to the piano wholeheartedly, to the point where Reginald and I enroll her in a music school run by American Joan Koenig.

When in Paris, do as the Parisians do, so we hire a French chef, Patrick Llorens, to cook our meals. Meanwhile, Christina has a French babysitter, Karine Atikossi, who speaks a little English.

During major holidays, Reginald flies our family back to the United States aboard the corporate jet and then repays TLC Beatrice for our trans-Atlantic flight. When the plane lands at New Jersey's Teterboro Airport, which is 12 miles from Manhattan, or at Orly Airport, which is eight miles outside of Paris, it's amazing to observe the long line of limousines waiting for the private jets that fly into those destinations.

When Leslie was accepted to Harvard College, we flew in the private jet from Paris to Boston to accompany her. On the return flight to Paris, Reginald was annoyed that I had tears in my eyes.

He didn't want me crying because he was fighting the feeling himself!

When the entire family is in Paris, Reginald, Leslie, and Christina love to tell jokes or solve math problems that start with, "Charlie works in a computer store. . . . " Every now and then, differences of opinion arise and conflicts need to be resolved. We Filipinos approach that by placing a premium on compromise and consensus. This is unlike Americans, who strike me as possessing a scorched-earth, zero-sum approach to conflict resolution.

In the grand scheme of things, these are minor quibbles. Since we've moved to Paris, I'm thrilled to see my daughters become citizens of the world and have come to admire their intelligence, confidence, poise, and kind hearts.

The four members of the Lewis family adore each other, irritate each other, laugh with each other, debate each other, and make each other proud.

In other words, we're a typical family, even if we hang out in Paris' 7th district and even if our head of household recently landed on *Forbes* magazine's list of 400 richest Americans.

Too bad no one ranks US couples who have the 400 most affectionate marriages because Reginald and I would be on that list, also. After more than two decades of being husband and wife, I know *exactly* where he lives. I know where he disappears to mentally during moments of self-doubt. I know the immense satisfaction he derives from his business achievements, and I know why he finds them gratifying.

Equally significant, Reginald has finally figured out where I live, which has made our time in Paris a real lovefest. A few weeks ago, he surprised me with tickets for the Vienna Philharmonic Orchestra and then whisked me to Vienna aboard his corporate jet for a romantic weekend.

Paris seems to have amplified the qualities that initially drew me to my husband, including his wonderful sense of humor and the inner romantic he hides from the rest of the world.

Reginald is wonderfully relaxed in Paris because he's treated as just another Parisian. When we traipse through Paris as a loving African-American/Filipino-American couple, my soulmate says he never sees the doubletakes he's come to expect in most US cities.

I love being in Paris with Reginald, who's constantly laughing and smiling and doesn't take his racism detector with him wherever he goes. It's a joy to see him saunter through the 7th district unencumbered by the weight of US bigotry.

Had I known Paris would agree with Reginald this way, filling our union with romance, tranquility, and mutual respect, I would have suggested that we move here long ago!

# 10

# LOIDA NEVER FAILS

**B**efore marrying Reginald, I tell him that while Filipinas may be kind-hearted and easy-going, don't make us jealous. I add that if he ever has a dalliance with another woman, I'd prefer not to know, because Philippine women are dangerous when we get angry.

I'm not stupid and know the male species a lot better than some people give me credit for. The other man in my life, Francisco J. Nicolas—a.k.a. Papa—has taught me well in this regard.

Like most people, I've come to regard my parents as quasi-immortals who'll always be there for me. So, I'm gutted when Papa suffers a serious heart attack in 1978.

As I've said, Papa and Reginald are a lot alike in that they're incredibly ambitious, industrious, and visionary. But Papa doesn't possess Reginald's brooding, fire-breathing intensity. In fact, my father is always seeking excuses to relax and have fun. Along with getting in 18 leisurely holes of golf every day, my father absolutely *loves* to dance.

He's always the first person to hit the dance floor and can be depended upon, as the saying goes, to dance like no one is looking.

He's a really, really good dancer too, to the point of being a bit of an exhibitionist. Whether he's doing the tango, cha-cha, or even a polka, my rotund Papa always leaves surprised onlookers cheering and applauding when he struts off the dance floor.

When I was 14, he brought ballroom dancers to our house in Sorsogon so my siblings and I could pick up the finer points of ballroom dancing. So, I can't believe it after I fly to the Philippines with Leslie for Christmas 1978, enter the living room of my family's house, and encounter my listless father sitting in a wheelchair. His speech is labored, and the left side of his body doesn't move properly.

As stunned as I am, Mama's had an even bigger surprise: She's learned for the first time that Papa's had a mistress for more than three decades. She never knew because I never told her about Nene Rustia, despite knowing about her. My brothers were also in on the secret, along with Mely, but who wants to break that kind of news to their mother?

After finding out and feeling utterly humiliated, the first thing Mama does is heatedly confront Nene. After cooling down, Mama makes a decision that makes me proud to this day: My mother allows Papa's mistress to come by our house once a week to visit my ailing father!

There was one occasion during the 1970s where I met Nene, a classy lady who's thin, attractive, light-skinned, very well put together, and fond of perfectly applied makeup.

Nene and the father of her four children got divorced during World War II, which was when she and Papa started their relationship. She's a businesswoman who owns a rooming house and, I think, sells textiles wholesale. My father helped launch her career as an entrepreneur.

Nene says she had an abortion after Papa got her pregnant, because she didn't want to complicate my father's life. Out of loyalty to my mother, I've had no contact with Nene, other than our one meeting. Still, I feel it's inappropriate of me to judge her because she's someone my father loves in a different way than he loves Mama.

I understand that sometimes a wife can't fully meet all of her husband's needs. And I appreciate that Nene didn't try to pressure my father into leaving my mother, and I respect that Nene loves Papa deeply and is able to give him happiness.

When Papa passes away on August 8, 1979, at the age of 70 following another heart attack, I beat myself up during the multihour flight from New York City to Manila. A few years earlier, when my father appeared to be slowing down mentally and was fleeced during a business deal, I presumptuously wrote Papa a letter advising him to step back and let my siblings play a more active role in his business endeavors.

Nene wrote me afterward that when the accomplished businessman got that letter from his know-it-all attorney daughter, it shattered his heart. Writing that missive was ridiculously high-handed and arrogant on my part, and I hope you've forgiven me, Papa. I regret that more than you know.

On the subject of forgiveness, as my family discusses my father's funeral arrangements and is waiting for me to arrive in the Philippines, Mama makes an explosive, last-minute decision to exclude Nene from Papa's funeral. My father has the last word here, because at that instant the lights in our home inexplicably go dark, then Papa's car mysteriously refuses to start.

## STEPPING OUT

Reginald, Christina, and I are all singing the praises of our French chef, Patrick Llorens, as our dinner dishes are cleared away inside our Paris apartment. Whatever Patrick puts his focus on—a formal four-course meal for 10, breakfast souffles, desserts, or a light dinner for three, like tonight—the man cooks it with aplomb.

Leslie's away at Harvard, but she's also a fan of Patrick's when she's home. Once the dishes have been whisked away, our maid sets two flutes of champagne on our dinner table, one in front of Reginald, one in front of me. If you can't beat 'em, join 'em, I say.

It feels wonderful to have my beloved around, because Reginald's been going to Manhattan for a month at a time to search for the next business deal. Then he comes to Paris for a month to be with me and the girls, along with visiting TLC Beatrice operating units in Ireland, Spain, Italy, and of course France.

As my husband and I sip champagne, we listen proudly as Christina smoothly practices a Beethoven piece on the brown concert piano in the living room. Christina manages to coax such rich, full-bodied tones out of that musical instrument! Our baby girl definitely has a gift for tickling the ivories, but I try not to make too much of a fuss over it.

I've seen that when kids get a sense their parents are keen on them doing something, sometimes they do the exact opposite just to get a rise out of Mom and Dad. That shouldn't be a problem with Christina, though, who plays the piano because she enjoys it, not because Reginald and I want her to. But she's sounding so good tonight that neither my husband nor I can resist the urge to clap lightly when she finishes, prompting a grin and an exaggerated curtsy before she heads off to bed.

God, thank you for the blessings you keep sending this family's way. Please don't let them stop, Lord!

"Babe, how did my favorite author do while I was in Manhattan?" Reginald asks, before taking a casual sip of champagne.

I love that "favorite author" moniker because I'm quite proud to have written a self-published book, *How the Filipino Veteran of World War II Can Become a US Citizen*. It's a do-it-yourself tome for Filipinos who fought with the US military in the Far East during World War II, but were denied US citizenship.

I'm currently writing a second book, *How to Get a Green Card*, which I had originally named *101 Legal Ways to Stay in the USA*, before rethinking the title.

Prior to kicking off my writing career, I told my man I needed an apartment that would serve as a writer's den, so with his consent I rented one for 3,000 francs a month. My driver ferries me to my writing spot, where I spend about five hours a day working on a little MacIntosh computer Leslie taught me how to use before she went off to Harvard. In light of the fact Reginald is subsidizing my writer's den, it feels good to show he's backed a winner.

"*Tres bien, tres bien* darling," I reply, puffing out my chest ever so slightly. "I should be able to put '*Green Card*' to bed in a few weeks."

"Awesome. I'm jealous."

"Why? Aren't you writing your autobiography, *Why Should White Guys Have All the Fun?*, in longhand?"

"Yep. Making good progress too."

"Maybe we'll wind up with the same publisher." I thought that might get a little laugh, but Reginald appears stern and unsmiling.

"Loida, I want you to know that I had dinner with Yvonne Powell (not her real name) while I was in New York," Reginald says nonchalantly. "I'd rather you hear it from me and not from somebody else."

Feeling as though I've just been kicked in the midsection, my heart sinks. Who else might I hear it from, aside from Yvonne? And why would that be? I plaintively pose these questions with my eyes because the link between my brain and my mouth has just short-circuited spectacularly.

I know Yvonne is single, beautiful, accomplished in her entertainment career, sexy, and Black. The green-eyed monster immediately rears its wretched, ugly head and starts going to town, as I struggle not to show a strong emotion one way or the other.

"Oh really? How is she?" I finally ask in what I hope sounds like a normal voice. I'm an acquaintance of Yvonne's and know that when she sees something she wants, she has zero qualms about going after it.

"She is fine." And with that, Reginald segues to another topic, to my towering irritation. His mouth is moving, and I hear his deep voice, but his words aren't registering with me right now.

Where my impressive self-control and discipline are coming from, I'm not sure. I just know I'm not going to sit here and grovel for additional details. So, I let my growling stomach speak for me, as it tussles with the French cuisine and champagne I'd found so delightful up till a few seconds ago.

Afterward, for the first and only time in my marriage, I lay beside Reginald in our bed and pray that he doesn't touch me. I'm hurt and angry enough to chomp his hand off.

Now that he's informed me of his "tryst" with Yvonne, my imagination tortures me with thoughts of the two of them together during those weeks he was in Manhattan.

I think I'll scream if one more Reginald-Yvonne scenario plays out in my head—it's driving me crazy! Whatever did or did not happen, fixating on the possibilities is pushing me toward an unhealthy place.

Along with the Yvonne situation, the rapid rise in the wealth, luxury, and privilege that I'm experiencing with Reginald is also making me uncomfortable. I don't want to delude myself into believing we're responsible for the blessings we're reaping, as opposed to a higher power.

I've been attending the only English-speaking Catholic Church in Paris, St. Joseph's Church, and read in the church bulletin that a prayer group is being formed that only meets on Fridays. I immediately sign up and find a group composed of about 15 women from different countries whose husbands are working in Paris.

I develop a very close friendship with Nora Brady, who's from Ireland and is always full of wise, practical observations when our prayer group convenes in a St. Joseph's Church classroom.

I confide in Nora that I'm feeling jealous, angry, and generally out of sorts because my imagination is torturing me. To put my emotions in context, I share with Nora what Reginald disclosed about his "affair" with Yvonne. One of the things I love about Nora is that she never pretends to have all the answers and carefully listens to what I have to say before responding.

"Loida, why don't you read the letter of St. Paul to the Corinthians that talks about what love is," she says calmly, following a moment of reflection.

When I get back to our apartment, I pull out my New International version of the Bible and read the first letter of St. Paul to the Corinthians, chapter 13, verses 4 to 8. I read it slowly, to best receive the passage's full impact.

> Love is patient.
> Love is kind.
> It does not envy.
> It does not boast.
> It is not self-seeking.
> It is not easily angered.

It keeps no record of wrongs.
It always protects.
It always trusts.
It always hopes.
It always perseveres.
Love never fails.

Wow!

I read it again, this time in prayer. And I insert myself into St. Paul's words.

Loida is patient.
Loida is kind.
Loida does not envy.
Loida does not boast.
Loida is not self-seeking.
Loida is not easily angered.
Loida keeps no record of wrongs.
Loida always protects.
Loida always trusts.
Loida always hopes.
Loida never fails.

The next time Reginald is in Manhattan for a month, I ponder, mull over, and meditate on those words, one sentence at a time.

And I make a point of remembering occasions when I was not patient.

When I was not kind.

When I was envious.

When I was boastful.

When I was self-seeking.

When I was easily angered. Oh yes.

When I kept multiple records of Reginald's wrongs. Oh yes.

When I did not protect him from my negative thoughts.

When I did not trust him to be faithful to me.

Lastly, when I failed him by not loving him unconditionally.

By the time he returns from New York, I'm transformed. I'm joyful and very happy to have him back. I no longer possess a drop of jealousy, envy, or the slightest bit of anger. I mentally incinerated a list of his wrongdoings that I had been accumulating. POOF!

He can do no wrong.

His words, even when harsh or judgmental or wrong, now roll off me like water off a duck's back.

I've fallen in love with my man all over again.

# 11

# SOME RAIN MUST FALL

**R**IIING! RIIING! RIIING!

Who's calling our Paris apartment at 2 a.m.? The phone in the master bedroom won't stop clanging until Reginald rolls over and snatches it off the hook.

"Hello?" he answers sleepily . . . "What?!"

Wide awake now, my spouse sits up in bed, the phone receiver pressed tightly to his ear. Judging from the startled look on Reginald's face and amount of time he spends silently listening, something terrible is happening. When he finally hangs up and turns to me, I hold my breath for a beat.

"Loida, Broadview is burning," he says in a flat voice.

"What?"

"They said that the fire began with a big blast, which was followed by another blast. . . ."

Reginald picks up the phone again and calls Leslie at Harvard. Simply by listening to what Reginald says, and how he says it, I can tell Leslie's as shocked as I am.

Next my husband calls his mother, Carolyn Fugett, in Baltimore. He tells Mom to alert her brother, Uncle Donald, a lifelong Baltimore City firefighter, that Reginald may need his expertise at East Hampton. Like me, my husband immediately suspects arson is behind the massive fire that's currently devouring our home.

I didn't want to further upset Reginald, but the first thing that came to my mind was an arsonist who resents seeing Black people prosper. I'll keep that to myself for the time being, so I don't wind up coping with a literal conflagration and a figurative one.

After hanging up with Mom, my beloved calls two TLC Beatrice executives also working in Paris, David Guarino and Kevin Wright. He asks them to book him the earliest available Concorde flight to New York, and to also direct the corporate jet to pick up Leslie in Boston and then whisk her to Long Island.

"Dear Lord, please protect our butler at Broadview, Lucien Stoutt, from all evil and danger," I silently pray. There's a chance Lucien's smoldering body may be in our East Hampton home because he sleeps in a section of the mansion that's over the garage.

The phone rings again—Reginald needs to leave immediately if he's to catch a pre-dawn flight to New York City. We're both in a state of disbelief as I give him a super-tight embrace in our foyer, right before he sprints down our second-floor hallway.

Once he's left, I stand in the eerily quiet foyer, praying for Lucien and recalling some of the incredible events and family activities Broadview has hosted from the time we bought it until this horrible day, November 6, 1991.

Reginald and I held our 20th anniversary celebration at Broadview. Last summer, it was the site of my mother's 80th birthday party, along with a shindig for Leslie where there were easily 300 Hampton teenagers in and around the house. Fun-filled Lewis-Fugett family reunions have been thrown at Broadview on the Fourth of July in 1988, 1989, 1990, and 1991.

My mind also flashes to the millions of dollars' worth of museum-quality artwork that Reginald has displayed in Broadview. Paintings by Black artists Vincent Smith, Ed Clark, Henry Taylor, as well as by

French artist André Fougeron, may be going up in smoke right this moment. Not to mention an exquisite sculpture of actor Paul Robeson that sprang from the fertile imagination of artist Jacob Epstein. No, this can't be happening . . . I'm sure I'll get a phone call informing me that Lucien is fine and the fire in our East Hampton dream home was extinguished before causing much damage.

Oh lord, I just remembered that we left 95% of our family photo albums in Broadview rather than drag them all the way to Paris. There's no way . . . it's fine, Loida, everything's fine. Be patient, trust in God's miracles, and be ready to receive the good news with a grateful heart.

The waiting is already unbearable before I leave the foyer, so I get on the phone and call the Philippines to let Mama and Mely know of the terrible scene unfolding in New York. My voice catches a couple of times, but I manage to keep it together while breaking the bad news to my mother and my sister. They're both subdued and valiantly try to come up with comforting words. They succeed too, after informing me they're far more worried about Lucien than Broadview and will be praying for his safety.

When Christina wakes up and I reveal the fate that's befalling our summer home in Amagansett, she doesn't say much afterward. Me either. What is there to say, really, as we sit helplessly on the other side of the Atlantic while our majestic Long Island home and possibly a Lewis family employee are being incinerated? Neither of us verbalize it, but it feels as though we're holding a long-distance deathwatch for Lucien and for Broadview.

Christina and I are both relieved when it's nearly time for her classes and we leave the apartment to head to her school. It's a timely distraction that couldn't come at a better moment. Unfortunately, it doesn't last long, and the unbearable suspense of not knowing what's going on with Lucien or Broadview drags on the rest of day and into the night.

Not till the following morning does Reginald inform me that our butler escaped with his life, thank God!

Lucien was helping his girlfriend, Rena Hewie, move to her new apartment in Long Island. They were on their way back to Broadview to spend the night, when she discovered she forgot to bring her work clothes. Once they returned to her apartment, Lucien suggested: "Let's just stay here, because I'm too tired to drive back to Broadview."

That casual decision may have ended up saving his life. Lucien confides later that Reginald greeted him with a scathing, "You f***ed up!" because Lucien's job entails staying at Broadview and keeping an eye on things.

As soon as Reginald and Leslie convene on our still-smoldering summer home, he immediately reaches out to his buddy and tennis partner, New York City Mayor David Dinkins, for help. Reginald points out that he's been a New York City resident and taxpayer since 1968, so could Dinkins please dispatch the city's most capable arson investigators out to Broadview?

David, who's played tennis with Reginald at Broadview and who's stayed at our Paris apartment, gladly complies with his good friend's request. David's investigators find the blaze appeared to originate in a wet bar on Broadview's first floor. When a section of the burning first floor fell into the basement below, it caused an oil tank situated in the basement to explode. And when the inferno reached another big oil tank on the other side of the basement, it also blew up.

That would account for the two blasts Reginald mentioned after getting off the phone and alerting me to the fire at Broadview. Local fire departments sent scores of firefighters to Broadview, but several hours passed before the flames were finally subdued. The room holding Reginald's pool table and the garden room were all that firefighters could save of the humongous Georgian mansion where my family and I spent so many happy, glorious days.

Along with Lucien's avoidance of the conflagration, the Broadview fire yields one other miracle: All of our photo albums were spared, but they'll have to undergo a special process to remove soot. I'm not sure whose call it was, but someone stashed all the family pictures in the same room where the pool table is located. Of course, many of the photographs were snapped at Broadview, enabling us to see our wonderful summer home in its former glory.

When Reginald returns to our Paris apartment a few days later, I meet him at the door, and we tightly embrace one another as we silently sob. Insurance will cover everything that was lost at Broadview, but it still feels like we've had a death in the family.

As a show of gratitude, Reginald sends Thanksgiving turkeys to all the firefighters who gave it their all to save our home.

## MORE DISTRESSING NEWS

A little more than a month after the fire, December 16, 1991, Mely calls me long-distance from Manila.

"Loida, Mama is in the hospital, and it's serious."

Goosebumps pop up on both my arms, while dread fills my heart. Noooo, not Mama!

"What's going on, Mely? I just spoke to Mama a week ago, about how much she loved her 80th birthday party at Broadview. She was fine then—is something wrong with her now!"

"Mama complained last Sunday that she was not feeling well. So, we brought her to the hospital, and the doctors thought it was a possible stroke. But by Tuesday they realized there had been a misdiagnosis. It wasn't a stroke; she has pneumonia, and it's already reached sepsis stage."

"Whoa, whoa! So, what happened, Mely? What's going on?"

"Loida, it does not look good. You better come as soon as you can,"

"Lord, please help Mama recover from her illness," I pray earnestly as I dial Reginald's number in New York.

"Darling, Mely just called to say Mama is very sick," I tell my husband without bothering to downplay my anxiety. "Pneumonia. I have to leave immediately."

"Of course, Loida. Ask Karine to stay with Christina. I'll come right away to be with her."

I quickly book a flight from Paris to Manila, and I pray incessantly during the 17-hour journey. "Lord, let me reach Manila on time so I can say goodbye to Mama." As I squirm and fidget in my airliner seat, for some reason my mind keeps dredging up a line from "The Rainy Day," a Henry Wadsworth Longfellow poem I learned in high school:

*Into each life some rain must fall.*

I could use some metaphorical raingear in light of Broadview and the serious malady that's imperiling Mama.

Following Papa's death in 1979, Mama sought solace in the Philippines' Born Again evangelical movement, which emphasizes the fundamentals of Christianity, along with maintaining a personal relationship with our Lord and Savior, Jesus Christ. In addition to facilitating a spiritual awakening in my mother, Born Again has done the same for my younger brother, Francis, and his wife, Ching.

Mama has invited all of her children, including me, to Born Again meetings. I attended one in Manila that featured an American pastor from California, Brother Tom Kowalski.

In the intervening years since Papa's passing, Mama has become much more spiritual and is a lot less likely to be angry and irritated when she encounters incompetence and dimwitted thinking. In fact, she's now so joyous and grateful about life's little blessings that "Praise the Lord!" is frequently on her lips.

My siblings and I are also used to hearing, "In the name of Jesus, devil, get out of here!" when Mama sees anything that could possibly lead to bodily harm or illness.

After what seems like days, the tires of my plane finally thump against the tarmac in Manila. Hoping against hope that Mama is still with us, I impatiently wait for the pilots to slow my aircraft down and then taxi toward the terminal, so I can get off of this thing. "God, please let me see my mother alive one final time!"

But when I finally see Mely in the airport terminal, her expression is beyond grim.

"Loida, *wala na si Mama* (Mama is gone). She died a few hours ago. I am so sorry you did not reach her alive."

"Oh my God, Mely! Oh my God!" Latching onto my sister, I unleash a torrent of tears onto her blouse. I'm too late! My mother leaves this earth on December 18, 1991, five days before my 49th birthday.

Lord, please safeguard Mama's soul and please grant her eternal peace.

## WAKING UP

Still reveling in the renewed commitment that my soulmate and I have to our marriage, and to one another, I wake up in Paris one morning to find the bedsheet under Reginald is sopping wet.

Clearly, he was sweating like mad as he slept—his skin still glistens with perspiration. Reaching across our bed, I grab Reginald's shoulder and give him a couple of gentle shakes.

"Darling!"

"Whaaaaat?"

His eyes fly open, focused first on me, and then on the wet silk flattened under his body. He turns on his side, props his head on his hand, and shoots me his sexiest smile.

"Of course I'm sweating, Babe," he says huskily, "I was dreaming about *you!*"

We both get a good laugh out of that. But there's nothing funny about the second time my beloved wakes up drenched in sweat. Nor is it vaguely humorous when it begins happening with increasing regularity throughout October 1992.

Unsurprisingly, Reginald refuses to allow night sweats to curtail his workaholic lifestyle. Because he owns and oversees a food empire scattered throughout France, Italy, Belgium, Thailand, Germany, Spain, and Norway, Reg is forever flitting across Europe at 45,000 feet, aboard his twin-engine, Bombardier Challenger jet.

But when my beloved starts having problems with the vision in his right eye, in addition to the mysterious perspiring, that catches his attention. Mine too.

A couple of weeks ago, as we're leaving one of Paris' premier opera houses, the Palais Garnier, and entering the backseat of our limo, Reginald accidentally brushes his head against the roof of the car.

WUMP!

"Are you okay, Darling?" I ask, reaching over to rub his forehead, near his hairline. Proud to a fault, my chagrined husband moves his head away from my hand. For my money, it's past time to make a doctor's appointment. The sweating and impaired vision aren't going to disappear magically.

For several moments the nightlights of Paris flash by without a word between my husband and me. Reginald Francis Lewis is his own man and does not like to be babied or pressured into decisions. But I think even he's starting to see that it's time to act.

"I think I'm going to fly to Manhattan for a 50th-birthday checkup," he finally says, trying to sound casual and indifferent. But I know Reginald, and hear a trace of concern in his voice. I lightly grab his right hand and stroke it lovingly.

It's been clear to me that something is amiss and needs to be addressed sooner, rather than later.

# 12

# LOSING MY
# SOULMATE

Ernest Hemingway once noted that "writing is rewriting." Meaning that tapping out spellbinding prose rarely comes easily to writers, including the great Hemingway.

In keeping with that tradition, I'm inside my Paris apartment busily tweaking some book passages that I've already written. *How to Get a Green Card* has been picked up by a publisher, and I want the manuscript to be as close to perfect as possible before I submit it.

It's 9 a.m., and Christina is at her École Active Bilange Jeannine Manuel international school, Leslie is at Harvard, and their dad is in Manhattan. Yesterday, December 7, 1992, was Reginald's 50th birthday, and I'll be hitting the Big-Five-Oh myself in a couple of weeks. When I was an undergraduate student, 50 seemed downright decrepit, but now that I've practically reached it, I feel like I'm just entering my prime. That's also how I view Reginald.

As I work on my Macintosh and sip morning coffee in the company of a writer's best friends, quiet and solitude, the phone rings in my little study, which is between Christina's bedroom and the master bedroom.

"Hello."

"Morning. How's everything?"

Keeping the phone to my ear, I clap my free hand over my mouth. I'm already detecting that something's out of kilter. Where's the electric "Hi, Babe!" that zings over the phone line and elevates my spirits? Reginald sounds robotic . . . but he's probably just tired.

"The doctor says it appears there's a lump in my brain. He's basing that on my symptoms and a preliminary exam."

Oh my God, no Reginald, oh my God. NO! My free hand falls from my mouth and brushes against my writing table.

"How could anyone—what doctor is saying this?"

"A Manhattan oncologist. I've gotten two second opinions and have a Christmas Eve biopsy scheduled."

My emotions are all over the map, while Reginald is strangely emotion-free and matter of fact. There's no weeping or self-pity, just a quasi-monotone indicating that he's come to grips with a terribly unsettling reality.

Taking a cue from the calm, dignified way he's handling himself, I resist an urge to pepper him with a million rapid-fire questions. That would only put my spouse under more stress.

"Christina and I are coming to New York. I just need to get a few things in order, and we'll be in the air tomorrow."

"I'll send the plane for you. Luv ya, Babe." Only when he utters those last words does my husband sound like his old self.

"I love you too, darling. We'll look into this—sounds like a misdiagnosis."

"Let's hope so."

We hang up, and I remain seated at my writing desk as paralyzing disbelief and numbness wash over me. Doctors make mistakes *all* the time, so how dare Reginald's physicians talk about brain tumors if my beloved still hasn't had a biopsy? Has he even been X-rayed?

Beyond that, how do I best facilitate a seamless transition from Paris to Manhattan for me and Christina? Think, Loida! Locating a pen and a sheet of lined, yellow legal paper on my desk, I try to write a to-do list that will enable me to fly to Manhattan, but my hand is quivering too much to write.

I can't think, and I can't write. No problem. God always has my back, so I'll pray.

"Father God, please give Reginald the strength and patience to overcome his illness," I say quietly. "Please cover my beloved with Your mantle of protection and heal him, Lord. In the mighty name of our Lord, Jesus Christ. Amen."

With my prayer ended, I immediately spring into action. I summon our housekeepers, Marlesa and Perfecto; our chef, Patrick; my chauffeur, Raymond; and Reginald's chauffeur, Patrick to the apartment. When everyone is present, I inform them that Monsieur Lewis is sick, and therefore Christina and I are heading back to the United States to be with him.

Too professional and discreet to inquire about the nature of Reginald's malady, all of them appear pained and shocked by the sudden turn of events. I begin limiting my eye contact, lest the emotion of the moment overwhelm me. That nearly happens anyway, because everyone is genuinely worried and wonderfully solicitous.

I tell everyone that Christina and I could use their help packing clothes and other essential items for us to take back to New York. And I assure them that I'll make sure no one is left in the lurch financially.

Next, I debate whether to immediately pull Christina out of school or let her finish the school day. I opt for the latter because things are going to be traumatic enough for my daughter as it is. I'd love for her to be able to say goodbye to her friends, but that can be accomplished via a long-distance call.

As for Leslie, I don't feel it's my place to break the news of Reginald's illness to her. I'll let him handle that as he sees fit.

Christina returns home to find me sweaty, wearing jeans and a T-shirt. A surprisingly large amount of work needs to take place before we're ready to leave this big 25-room dwelling tomorrow. Realistically, I can't see us being finished then, even with the staff's help.

"What's going on, Mom?" Christina asks with alarm, gesturing at the boxes and luggage scattered throughout our place.

"Honey, I found out today that your father has a medical problem. We need to be with him in Manhattan to help him get well."

"So, we're going to be living in New York again?"

"Yes, sweetheart. We're returning to the United States."

Christina's mind is clearly moving a mile a second, but to my relief, she asks no further questions. That way, there's no need for me to launch into a discussion about brain cancer. Reginald isn't even 100% certain that's what he's confronting.

As I look at my concerned 12-year-old, my maternal side says, "What in the world are you waiting for, Loida? Give your baby girl a big hug—she needs one!" Meanwhile, my cerebral side chimes in with: "Why would you want to scare Christina unnecessarily by giving her a bear hug? All that will do is alarm her, when you're not even sure what's actually wrong with Reginald!"

Feeling surprisingly awkward and tentative, I do nothing, beyond dropping items into an open box that's going to be shipped back to New York. I can feel Christina glancing at me—am I handling this well? No, I'm not. Sorry, baby, I'm pretty out of sorts right now and trying to muddle my way through this.

I'll get better at this, I promise. Actually, I won't need to, because modern medicine—and God—are going to figure out what's wrong with your father and fix it.

Joined by members of the Lewis family staff, Christina and I wind up working till about 2 a.m. Much of my time is spent on the phone, calling the school Christina attended in Manhattan to let them know she'll be returning and alerting the members of my church prayer group that we'll be away in Manhattan for an indeterminate amount of time.

I also take the time to show the Lewis family staffers what needs to stay in our Paris apartment and what needs to remain behind, as I help pack boxes.

Everyone is very subdued and quiet in our 25-room apartment, including me. Since I see no sense in everyone pulling an all-nighter, I eventually thank the staff for their help and concern and ask them to return in a few hours. After everyone leaves, Christina and I hit the sack.

Surprisingly, mercifully, I fall asleep quickly, without tossing and turning, as I fixate on Reginald and his medical dilemma. I pray to a loving God and am certain He won't allow any misfortune to befall my husband or my family or me.

Miracles happen and, as Psalm 145 accurately notes, my God is "gracious, and full of compassion; slow to anger, and of great mercy."

Lord, have mercy on my beloved!

## A Bogus Celebration After Devastating News

On the last day of 1992, Reginald and I are throwing a New Year's Eve black-tie dinner at our new apartment on 834 Fifth Avenue, across from Central Park. Reginald's mother, Carolyn Fugett, is up from Baltimore, along with her husband, Jean Fugett, Sr. Other members of the Baltimore clan at the dinner are Reginald's brother Jean Fugett, Jr., and his wife, Carlotta; brother Tony Fugett and wife, Trittye; sister Rosalyn Fugett and her spouse, Elliott Wiley; and sister Sharon Fugett. Rounding out the group are our daughters, Leslie and Christina.

Everyone is over the moon when it comes to the culinary creations of our chef, Dalma Walker, who's made a turkey dinner with all the trimmings.

I'm smiling and playing the gracious hostess, engaging in small talk, chuckling at joke punchlines, making sure everyone has enough to eat and drink. I deserve an Academy Award nomination—yesterday Reginald went to Memorial Sloan Kettering, where the city's top neurosurgeon performed a biopsy to see if my beloved has brain cancer.

The results came back positive. So, 24 hours later, Reginald and I are trying our best to act as though we never received the previous day's horrific news. This is easily the most bizarre, whacko New Year's Day ever. My man and I are the only people at the dining room table who know his heartbreaking secret, although part of Reginald's head has been shaved to accommodate the biopsy.

I'm sure someone at the table has probably noticed his altered hairline by now. What no one does see is how Reginald and I stealthily glance across the table at one another, silently communicating our love and support. The other thing that passes between us when our eyes meet is ironclad resolve—this cancer is in for one helluva fight.

While we have our private meeting of the minds within the framework of a family gathering, we're fielding compliments left and right on our spectacular new home. No one has any inkling what an incredibly low priority 834 Fifth Avenue is for us at the moment.

Still, we respond with a smile and a heartfelt "Thank you!" every time praise comes our way. Hands-down, it is the most surreal dinner of my life.

Sharp-eyed table guests would have noted that Reginald said grace this evening. A marked departure from our usual mealtime MO, because my spouse always allows me to bless the table before meals, followed by his mother.

After the main course is finished and our housekeepers begin clearing plates to make way for dessert, Reginald and I excuse ourselves to attend a black-tie reception upstairs in Lawrence and Mary Rockefeller's tri-level penthouse. The exceedingly gracious Rockefellers have about 12 couples milling around by the time we get there.

We don't stay long because we want to go back to our apartment and watch New Year's fireworks explode over Central Park with our family. Once under way, the display is festive and spectacular, but it doesn't ease the sense of dread I'm beginning to feel.

Still, as 1993 rolls in, the New Year finds me quietly, fervently beseeching the Lord to please bring healing to my beloved. In Jesus's name, amen!

## THE END COMES

It's been nine days since we celebrated New Year's Day. The Philippine faith healer I flew in from Manila to see Reginald just left 834 Fifth Avenue a few minutes ago, after wasting our time and money with his so-called psychic surgery.

I'd give anything for Reginald to opt for radiation or chemotherapy, Western medicine's go-to weapons for fighting cancer. But my husband has clearly stated that those options are off the table because he feels they'll hasten the erosion of his brain function. In fact, his ability to move the right side of his body and the vision in his right eye have declined dramatically since my spouse's biopsy.

My vibrant man, who was always on the move—whether teaching the girls how to ride bicycles or waging one of his epic tennis matches—now needs help from his brother, Tony, to get around. As much as anything, that underlines how uncompromising Reginald's foe is.

One night, a point comes when just the two of us are in our new home. We've gone into Reginald's study and are near an impressive bookcase full of tomes he can no longer stand up and grab, due to brain cancer.

"Loida, I need to share something," Reginald says slowly. "I had an affair, and it's definitely not something I'm proud of. I thought you should know."

I walk behind the French desk where my husband is seated, bend down so that we're cheek-to-cheek and hug him. "I know, Darling. As far as I'm concerned, you can do no wrong." Reginald raises his left hand, closes his eyes and gently caresses my face.

He understands that my love is unconditional, and that's all that matters. We spend several minutes in total silence, appreciating that we've been blessed to share a relationship for the ages.

The next day, Reginald, Tony, and I find ourselves in the living room of 834 Fifth Avenue, earnestly discussing alternative cancer treatments that haven't been approved by the US Food and Drug Administration.

The three of us are on the exact same page: We're going to defeat this dreadful disease, by any means necessary. Period.

Prior to calling on the faith healer, I had been in contact with a Chinese physician in Chinatown who recommended an herbal concoction he claimed could arrest my spouse's cancer. If it didn't work, Reginald would fall into a coma, the doctor cautioned, before adding: "It should work. It's worth a try."

So, I go to Chinatown, purchase the needed herbs and roots, and bring them back to Fifth Avenue for our chef, Dalma, to boil them and then put them in a blender. When Dalma's finished, what results is a glass full of unattractive brown liquid that looks like it oozed from a New York City sewage pipe. I present it to Reginald, who chugs a little of the special formula, wrinkles his nose, and simply growls, "Awful!!"

Reginald quaffs several glasses of the nasty brown elixir for a few days, before giving up.

After putting our heads together, Reginald, Tony, and I come up with a Canadian alternative treatment we feel might be worth a try. It involves injecting massive doses of vitamin C into cancer patients. Reginald and Tony are doing most of the conversing because I'm slowly falling off the alternative-treatment bandwagon.

I have a growing sense that if radiation and chemotherapy aren't options, we need to focus solely on God's ability to cure Reginald as opposed to seeking manmade solutions. It's becoming more and more clear to me that my beloved's fate is in the Almighty's hands. As a result, I have never prayed as intently as during the first weeks of January 1993.

TLC Beatrice's twin-engine corporate jet is called into service to ferry Reginald, his mother's youngest sister, Aunt Beverly, and me to Toronto, where a clinic specializing in the vitamin C regimen is located. Tony and his wife, Trittye, will join us in Toronto a few days after we get there.

During the short plane ride to Toronto, I begin experiencing an unwelcome new emotion—desperation. I'm working overtime to stomp out this feeling and eliminate it from my psyche, but I have to admit that my faith is being shaken by the inexorable decline in the condition of my husband, who now needs a wheelchair to get around. My pitched internal battle makes for an unsettling journey to Canada, especially when it's imperative that I appear rock-steady and unflappable in front of my spouse. I'm hoping for the best and am begging God for a positive outcome, so a sense of foreboding is the last thing I need right now.

The three of us check into the Fairmont Hotel in Toronto, and Beverly immediately begins arranging for Reginald to have a session where a massive dose of vitamin C will be injected into his body via intravenous drip. Canadian health authorities have conducted studies indicating that vitamin C destroys tumor cells while sparing healthy tissue.

For four consecutive days, Reginald and I drop by the clinic so he can be hooked to an IV that delivers vitamin C into his system. After the sessions, we head back to the hotel and watch the inaugural activities of president-elect Bill Clinton, who will be sworn in on January 20.

"I could have gone that route," Reginald says one day as we're watching television, meaning he could have had a successful political career.

"Darling, Bill Clinton has always focused on a political life in order to serve people. You set yourself up to excel in the financial world, and you've done it!"

My beloved smiles and says, "You must admit, it has been quite a ride, Loida. I disproved the lie. . . ."

He doesn't need to continue. We both know exactly what he's talking about: TLC Beatrice has become the first Black-owned business with more than $1 billion in annual revenue. That's an indisputable fact that the naysayers can't ignore.

For the first time in days Reginald smiles, which warms my heart. And we share a private laugh later when he asks me to sashay across the floor of our hotel room in my high heels. The ultimate man's man, Reginald has always loved how heels accentuate my calves.

I'm thrilled that the love of my life still appreciates my feminine looks, and I embrace him lovingly when I lie beside him in bed.

On the evening of Saturday, January 16, Tony—who's an absolute godsend—comes by my hotel room and helps his brother to take a shower. Afterward, as Reginald is sitting in his wheelchair watching TV, he calls out to me.

"Loida!"

"Yes, Darling?"

"Something's going on with my eyes. It's like . . . someone's pulling a shade down over them."

"Can you still see?"

"Yes."

"Should I call the clinic?"

"No. That's not necessary."

Both of us are aware that Reginald's body is getting progressively weaker. His statement is almost a tacit acknowledgment that the vitamin C regimen isn't working as advertised.

On the morning of Sunday, January 17, Reginald awakens drenched in sweat, cradling his head in both hands. "My head hurts," he moans plaintively, as I spring out of bed and use the phone in our room to call Tony, who's next door.

After alerting Reginald's brother, I try to get in touch with the clinic's attending physician, so I can get him to visit our hotel room. A receptionist says my best bet is to try the emergency doctor who's on-call. Trying to ignore my rapidly growing panic, I call a Filipina nurse I befriended when Reginald and I first arrived at the clinic. She apologetically informs me that no one is available to come to my hotel room.

As we're speaking, Reginald collapses onto his drenched pillow and loses consciousness. By this time, Tony is in our hotel room and immediately calls Toronto's equivalent of 911. An ambulance appears at the hotel within minutes and whisks Reginald to a nearby hospital.

Please, Lord, please rescue my beloved!

As Trittye, Beverly, Tony, and I sit in a hospital waiting area, anxiously awaiting word on Reginald's condition, we're approached by a physician.

"I'm sorry. Your husband has suffered a massive brain hemorrhage," the doctor tells me somberly, never averting his unblinking gaze. "Unfortunately, it's caused irreversible damage."

I don't know why, but his words have eroded every ounce of denial and avoidance I'd built up in my brain, perhaps due to self-preservation. At that exact instant, it finally hits me: My beloved is going to die!

"NO!" I cry out. "NO! Oh Lord, have mercy, have mercy, have mercy, have mercy!" How is this even possible, Lord God? You have promised to hear the cry of the brokenhearted. Where are You, oh Lord?

My emotions gush like water cascading from a ruptured dam, rendering me totally incapacitated. I'm not in control of my body as sob after sob wells up from what seems like an endless reservoir of pain.

Maybe Tony or Beverly or Trittye can address what I said and did right after hearing that horrible news—I honestly can't tell you. I just know that my Superwoman façade shatters into a billion microscopic pieces and it feels as though my life force is exiting my body.

Following an emotional outpouring that leaves my blouse wet with tears, the doctor escorts me to Reginald's hospital room.

My beloved is in a hospital bed with a huge breathing tube down his throat and his eyes closed, his body under what looks like miles of wiring and plastic tubing. Sensors on his head and chest and even his fingertips, lead to beeping machines that display Reginald's heart rate, brain activity and even the oxygen level in his blood.

Basically in shock, barely able to speak, I decide on the spot that I'm not going to interact with my husband as if he's in a coma. I haven't done that since I met him 25 years ago: Why start now?

"Darling, do you want to stay in this Canadian hospital?" I ask. "Or should we bring you to New York?"

Incredibly, I see his head make a tiny up and down movement, as though he's nodding in the affirmative. A miracle.

"We're moving my beloved to New York," I inform Tony and Beverly, right before requesting last rites for my soulmate. Incredibly, an African-born, Black Catholic priest appears and administers to Reginald what Catholics call extreme unction, or a final anointing. Another miracle!

In light of Reginald's precarious medical state, he could easily pass away during the flight from Canada to the United States. Somehow, most of the medical equipment he's attached to is unhooked, with the exception of his oxygen tank. My beloved is bundled against the blisteringly cold Canadian weather outside the hospital, and he's placed aboard his jet, along with a medical technician.

Leslie is waiting for us when the plane arrives in Teterboro Airport, in New Jersey. My daughter and I refuse to get into a waiting limo driven by John Botha, who's from Ghana and serves as my husband's chauffeur in New York. Not wishing to leave Reginald in the company of strangers once he's transferred to an ambulance, Leslie and I both hop in.

"Darling, we're back in the United States," I tell my soulmate as I chat with him the entire time. "We made it back to the States and are headed to Memorial Sloan Kettering in Manhattan."

I'm not sure if I'm talking to console myself at this point, but I have no intention of stopping. During the entire trip from Teterboro into Manhattan, I speak to Reginald as if he's conscious and responsive.

Nor do I leave Reginald's side after he's successfully transferred to Sloan Kettering and connected to an oxygen line to keep him alive. I maintain a nonstop vigil at his bedside, red-eyed and continually sobbing from a broken heart. I should probably leave the hospital and console our children. . . . I just can't.

Leslie and Christina are being tended to by a host of relatives, primarily Reginald's mother.

New York State policy dictates that after a person dies, their estate can't be touched until a Surrogate Court determines how much needs to be paid in estate taxes. Always looking ahead, Reginald arranged for $2 million to be transferred to my bank account, so that if anything happens to him, I can deal with expenses until the estate-tax situation can be resolved.

The bank transfer is executed on the morning of Tuesday, January 19, 1993. That afternoon, around 3 p.m., one of Reginald's nurses pulls me aside for a private chat.

"Mrs. Lewis, your husband's vital signs are slowing," she explains gently. "The end is near."

In the company of Leslie, Reginald's mother, and his brothers and sisters, I recite Psalm 23 in a quiet, wavering voice beside my husband's hospital bed. "The Lord is my shepherd. I shall not want. He makes me to lie down in green pastures. He leads me beside still waters. He restores my soul. Though I walk through the valley of the shadow of death, I feel no evil for Thou are with me. . . ."

After reciting the entire Psalm, I tell Reginald:

"It is okay for you to go, my darling! We will be alright. Do not worry about Leslie and Christina. We will be alright. Goodbye, my darling. I love you."

Around 3:30p.m., my soulmate departs this earth.

Lord, Lord, why have You abandoned me?

# 13

# UNFINISHED BUSINESS

"In the midst of winter, I have finally learned that there was in me an invincible summer."

—Albert Camus

I've spent most of 1993 in shock, a total basket case who's grateful to Mom for coming from Baltimore and staying with me in Manhattan for six months after my beloved Reginald passed away.

It feels as though my heart has been carved out, squeezed bone dry, and then placed back into my chest, which does nothing to stem my tears—I bawl every time I think of my darling Reginald, or hear Louis Armstrong warbling *What a Wonderful World,* my husband's favorite song.

One night as I'm lying in bed weeping, waiting for sleep to bring relief, I feel something touch my leg! It's Gilbert, the golden Labrador retriever that Reginald bought to keep him and Christina company in Paris after Leslie went off to Harvard. Gilbert slowly lays his paws on my waist, as if to say, "Do not weep. I am here with you!"

On that night at least, gentle Gilbert's presence helps me sleep better. Reginald undoubtedly sent him to soothe my raw, aching heart.

Compounding my misery is the fact that I'm living at 834 Fifth Avenue, which is full of magnificent artwork and antique French furniture that Reginald alone selected. I confess to his mother that I feel fraudulent living in a dream house my beloved spent good money to have renovated in record time but was only able to reap a month's worth of enjoyment from.

"Loida, just think of it as him having his arms around you in this house," Mom says. "He meant for you and the girls to live here, remembering him."

Those sage words mollify me. Yes, I can imagine that. Still, accepting that my soulmate is no longer with me is something I'm starting to wonder if I can accomplish.

Mom is one of the wisest people I've ever encountered and really should have been a teacher. She's an amazingly patient, nurturing soul who loves to instruct by using hypothetical scenarios. She'll slowly lay out Option A, B, and C and will then ask what you think the outcome from each is likely to be. This makes whomever she's talking to feel as though they've solved their own problem, even though Mom knew the answer before the conversation started.

Wise, wise woman. I love Mom in equal measure to my biological Mama in the Philippines.

Even though I'm having trouble understanding why God removed Reginald from my life, I still attend St. Vincent Ferrer, a Roman Catholic church a few blocks from 834 Fifth Avenue. During Holy Mass on Sunday, the priest starts saying the Lord's Prayer and I recite it along with the rest of the congregation. But when "Thy Kingdom come, Thy will be done" arrives, I can't get "Thy will be done" to leave my mouth.

With tears of anger and frustration sliding down my cheeks, I quietly implore God to give me the strength to live life without my beloved.

Almost half a year to the day after Reginald made his transition, I awaken to find brilliant sunlight streaming into our master bedroom.

The curtains to the room, which fronts Center Park, are drawn down at night, and I pull them up after I rise in the morning.

Did someone enter my bedroom and raise the curtains without awakening me?

Shielding my eyes, I roll out of bed and ask Mom, my housekeeper Estela Ylagan, Leslie—who's home from Harvard for the summer—and Christina whether they moved the curtains? Puzzled denials abound. Well, did Gilbert rise up on his hind legs and manipulate my bedroom curtains?

Then, I get it. No matter who did it, God is sending me a message: "It's time to pull back the curtains shrouding me in gloom, so I can let in some cleansing sunshine."

Thus, I start on the road to recovery. As I make my uphill climb, I'm sustained by words from the Good Book.

In particular, the Prophet Isaiah 41:10 gives me great comfort: "Do not be afraid for I am with you."

Isaiah 49:15 accelerates my recovery, too: "Can a mother forget the baby at her breast? Though she may forget, I will not forget you."

And Isaiah follows with: "I have engraved you on the palms of My hands."

I've reached out my hand to God and, after He grabs it and lifts me up, I'm finding I can walk with God beside me!

With my badly damaged psyche finally on the mend, my first responsibility is Leslie and Christina, whom I'm now a mother and a father to.

Because I've yet to see Christina cry since her father's death, I make a concerted effort to find a child psychiatrist who's both Black and female. After I hit paydirt and tell the physician about Christina, she explains that young children sometimes postpone their grieving following a traumatic event like the death of a parent.

The doctor explains that the mind of someone who's 12, like Christina, may shift into self-protection mode due to an inability to completely process what has transpired. Christina's mourning for Reginald might not occur until she's an adult, the psychiatrist adds.

She expresses an interest in speaking with Christina, but I nix that because of my daughter's youth. Letting the two of them engage might have helped Christina clarify her thoughts and feelings about her father's demise, but I didn't do it.

After her father died, Leslie returned to Harvard to take an exam in the middle of her sophomore year. She had to deal with her pain away from home, and I'm grateful she was able to do this in the company of classmate Gavin Sword, a Canadian who's Leslie's boyfriend. Gavin provided a shoulder to cry on while Leslie was grieving for her father and simultaneously juggling the demands of schoolwork.

After some reflection, I've admitted to myself that I'm reluctant to have an intimate conversation with Leslie about her father's demise.

As for Christina, I'm able to get her permanently re-enrolled in the Dalton School, which is where she was studying before we moved to Paris. Although Christina knows and speaks French like a Parisian after five years of life in Paris, the only foreign language Dalton is offering to seventh-graders is Spanish, so I hire a Spanish-language tutor so my baby can get caught up with the rest of her classmates.

Sadly, I'm clueless about the emotional toll she's undergoing during this time of profound sorrow and intense grief in her young life and am also unsure to what degree Leslie has been devastated by Reginald's tragic passing. I deeply regret not being more in sync with their emotional wounds, or their recoveries.

This is partially due to the fact that I'm now laser-focused on completing projects Reginald was robbed of an opportunity to finish. Along those lines, my top priority right now is getting his autobiography completed. I have no doubt my man's legacy has the ability to spur others to greatness.

## DOCUMENTING HIS LEGACY

Before he was overtaken by his cancer, Reginald filled several legal pads with engaging recollections about his life and accomplishments. He gave his neat cursive to secretaries Fay Jenkins and Nora Willis, so they could create typed documents. Reginald also recorded some of his thoughts on audio tape that he had secretary Deidra Wilson transcribe.

In terms of a title for his book, my beloved opted to go with *Why Should White Guys Have All the Fun?* That stems from a remark he made as a five-year-old after his grandparents noted that in Jim Crow Baltimore, the most desirable homes and jobs always went to Whites.

Detail-oriented to a fault, Reginald even shared with me a color photograph he wanted to grace the cover of his autobiography: It depicted him holding a cigar and practically oozing self-assurance.

"Darling, you look arrogant in that photo!" was my candid assessment.

"That's the idea," he countered with a twinkle in his eyes and a smile that accentuated his lovable dimples.

I need a writer who can accomplish the researching, interviewing, and writing necessary to finish Reginald's biography. With that in mind, I reach out to Butch Meily, a Filipino executive who oversees public relations for TLC Beatrice. Butch and I conclude that an African American is needed, to imbue Reginald's book with the kind of nuance he would have striven for.

Butch identifies seven potential writers, and after interviewing them all, we select *Washington Post* columnist Cortland Milloy. Courtland is a friend of one of Reginald's brothers, Jean Fugett, Jr., a Baltimore attorney who formerly played tight end for the Washington Redskins and who worked as a *Washington Post* reporter during the NFL's offseason.

Jean is also TLC Beatrice's acting chief executive officer, in accordance with a corporate leadership structure Reginald put together during his final days.

Courtland and Butch board TLC Beatrice International Holdings' jet in New Jersey and fly off to Europe, where Courtland visits operating units in Dublin, Brussels, and Barcelona. The goal is to let Courtland grasp the scope of Reginald's business empire. So that Courtland can appreciate the lifestyle Reginald enjoyed, I have dinner with him at my family's Paris apartment, along with Butch.

After three months of working on the book, Courtland decides he no longer wants to finish my beloved's autobiography. I'm extremely disappointed and annoyed because my goal is to have Reginald's autobiography on bookshelves by the first anniversary of his death, January 19, 1994.

But, as Reginald was so fond of noting, it's best to always have a Plan B, in case Plan A goes sideways. Fortunately, I happen to have a Plan B that my brother-in-law, Elliott Wiley, helps me execute.

Under Elliott's direction, we create *Reginald Lewis: A Tribute*, a 210-page hardcover book comprised primarily of pictures and remarks from three ceremonies: Reginald's January 23, 1993, funeral in Baltimore; a Manhattan memorial service that took place at Riverside Church two days later; and the dedication of the Reginald F. Lewis International Law Center on Harvard Law School's campus, on April 23, 1993.

The Harvard dedication stemmed from a $3-million gift my beloved made to the school, philanthropy that was panned in some quarters because he gave far less to two historically Black colleges and universities, Howard University and Reginald's undergraduate alma mater, Virginia State University.

I like the Reverend Jesse Jackson's response during remarks he made at my husband's Manhattan memorial service.

> Reggie gave money to Virginia State, to Howard, and Harvard, and some have questioned publicly why Reggie would give three million dollars to Harvard. Because he got three-million worth from Harvard! He wanted to buy a seat at the captain's table and eat where the captains ate and have more than the appetizer, but have equity at the table. And so he bought some space at the Harvard table. It was his sense of class and touch and making room for ongoing generations.

*Reginald Lewis: A Tribute* will enable me to have a book by the first anniversary of Reginald's transition. But I'm still determined to finish his autobiography. I know in my heart that readers of his incredible story, especially people of color, will be inspired to shoot for the American Dream themselves.

So, Butch and I are back to square one. No writer. No book.

Our second choice is Jonathan Hicks, a *New York Times* reporter who wrote a feature article on Reginald when he first acquired Beatrice International Foods. Like Reginald, Jonathan belongs to the Kappa Alpha Psi Fraternity, so by all appearances he seems an excellent fit.

But when Jonathan is approached, he turns down the offer. Probably because he's too close to his frat brother, in light of the fact that he and Reginald became very good friends.

Our third choice is *USA Today* writer Blair S. Walker. The day that Reginald died, Blair wrote an obituary in his newspaper's Money section that was accompanied by a huge photo of Reginald.

"I knew I would write his book!" is Blair's reaction when I call to inform him that Butch and I have chosen him to finish Reginald's biography. Like Reginald, Blair is from Baltimore and has a law degree.

After Blair takes a leave of absence from *USA Today*, my first order of business is to introduce him to Reginald's family. So, I call Mom, her husband, Jean Fugett, Sr., and Reginald's brothers, sisters, uncles, and aunts to let them know Blair will be contacting them about Reginald. I also provide Blair with the names of classmates, colleagues, and friends, in addition to news clippings and other materials for his research, including the autobiographical material produced by my beloved.

The literary agent attached to the project, Michael Cohn, is very pessimistic that an autobiography about a deceased Black businessman will do well, but Blair, Butch, and I overlook his negative comments and keep pressing forward.

*Why Should White Guys Have All the Fun?* winds up being published by John Wiley & Sons, and I'm able to get a copy prior to the book's official December 1995 date. I spend a long time admiring the "arrogant" picture of cigar-smoking Reginald Lewis that we found so amusing in Paris. This book has been such a major obsession of mine that actually holding it gives me a nearly palpable sense of relief.

I pray that my beloved finds *Why Should White Guys Have All the Fun?* worthy of his legacy. For my money, a 1,000-page tome couldn't begin to capture my man's force-of-nature personality, but John Wiley & Sons would likely view things differently.

The launch for Reginald's book takes place on the 48th floor of 9 West 57th Street, inside a cavernous, 35,000-square-foot suite of offices that used to be occupied by RJR Nabisco. Five years earlier, Reginald negotiated a discounted rent for what remained of RJR Nabisco's five-year lease, following the corporation's purchase by Kohlberg Kravis Roberts & Co.

*Why Should White Guys Have All the Fun?* becomes a *Business Week* magazine bestseller and generates robust sales.

As I had hoped, I've met scores of ambitious men and women who tell me Reginald's book altered their approach to their corporate careers or else provided the final nudge they needed to test the waters of entrepreneurship.

I'm sure this delights Reginald to no end.

## MOVING ON

After our sprawling summer home on Long Island, Broadview, burned to the ground in November 1991, Reginald and I discussed whether we should look for a replacement summer home in Europe or find another one in the United States.

After giving the matter additional thought, we looked at one another and said, "Why move? We both like the Hamptons!"

So, Reginald reached out to Ed Pétri, his real estate broker, to find a large East Hampton rental home for the summer of 1992. My husband chose an oceanfront, five-bedroom summer house with a guest house and a heated swimming pool that was located on West End Road in East Hampton Village. That's where we held our annual family reunion, but afterward Reginald and Ed began looking at properties that were for sale.

One that he particularly liked, "Daddy Warbucks," was on the market that summer, and we visited it a few times.

If you comb through East Hampton Village's property records, I guarantee you will not find a parcel or a structure named Daddy Warbucks. That sobriquet came from the fertile imagination of my oldest daughter, Leslie, in 1982 when Columbia Pictures released the movie *Annie*.

We trekked regularly to East Hampton as a family that year, thanks to Reginald's purchase of our Springy Banks summer home. During one of those East Hampton visits, Leslie viewed and thoroughly enjoyed *Annie* at the East Hampton Cinema. One of the main characters in the film, Daddy Warbucks, owned a massive three-story mansion that clearly made quite an impression on Leslie.

After leaving the theater and spotting a huge summer home on Lily Pond Lane that was perched on the highest oceanside bluff in the area, Leslie gleefully announced: "There's Daddy Warbucks!" Our family began calling the house on Lily Pond Lane Daddy Warbucks from that point forward.

Fast-forward to summer 1992, and Daddy Warbucks is on the market. After ogling the house from afar for the better part of a decade, my beloved puts in a $12-million bid on the property, and all four of us visit the house several times. The girls and I love it, because thanks to the elevated plot of land the house sits on, you can look down and see its huge swimming pool, along with a panoramic view of the Atlantic Ocean.

After Reginald submitted his bid for $12 million, real estate broker Ed Petri returned bearing bad news: David Geffen, who'd recently sold his interest in Geffen Records to SONY for nearly $1 billion, outbid Reginald by $1 million.

An astute businessman who tried not to develop emotional attachments that might cause him to pay too much for things, Reginald told the broker: "I'm not getting into a bidding war over the house. He can have it."

Although Reginald wanted the house badly, he let it go. The following year, 1993, my beloved passed away.

When summer rolls around, broker Ed Petri comes to me with a surprising news—Daddy Warbucks is on the market again! After protracted negotiations with property owner Maggie Minskoff, David Geffen has walked away from the deal.

Certain that Reginald is in heaven and working overtime so his family can finally acquire a summer home that we unanimously loved, I'm ecstatic.

"It's destined for the Lewis family to move in," I tell Ed Petri. "I'll match the $13 million that David Geffen offered, but under one condition—I want to meet Mrs. Minskoff."

I don't mention to Ed that I don't have the cash to buy Daddy Warbucks because Reginald's estate is currently tied up by New York Surrogate Court, but I'll figure out something. Details, details.

For the time being, I just want Maggie to get to know me, so I can assure her that I'll cherish and respect the house that she and her family have lived in since her late husband, Jerry Minskoff, bought it at auction in 1968. It had been rumored that David Geffen intended to destroy the house and build a mansion.

Along with needing to convince Maggie to give me a year to raise $13 million, I need to sweeten my offer with an inducement no other bidder would think of. That may be linked to the fact that Maggie's been renting out Daddy Warbucks to the same family for the last five years, with the stipulation that she be allowed to live in a small cottage on the property.

The two of us hit it off immediately at the Harvard Club, a Manhattan meeting spot that was one of Reginald's favorites. Maggie is in the theater business and used to be an actress. In light of my love of Broadway and off-Broadway plays, we have a lot to discuss as we break the ice.

Once the niceties have been dispensed with, I lay my proposal on the table: I'll meet her $13 million asking price, but she has to give me a year to raise the cash. In return, after we close the deal and the property is in my possession, I'll let her stay in the cottage for three years rent-free.

She agrees with my proposal on the spot!

I schedule a meeting with my private banker at JPMorgan, Robert Simon, who says I can get a mortgage for $13 million from JPMorgan. "How do you intend to pay us back?" Rob wants to know in true banker fashion. Time to get creative again.

I share with Rob that I don't need all of Daddy Warbuck's 11 acres, and can easily sell five undeveloped acres on one side of the house. Meanwhile, the house that burned—Broadview—has 12 acres I can sell, plus I'll be getting insurance money for Broadview, since officials have deemed the fire accidental.

That's enough to convince JPMorgan to greenlight my mortgage.

On February 13, 1995, Maggie Minskoff sells me Daddy Warbucks, then JPMorgan gives her $13 million and places a $13-million mortgage on the property. After I receive an insurance payment for Broadview, sell its 12 acres of land and six acres from the Daddy Warbucks property, I'm able to pay back JPMorgan and own Daddy Warbucks free and clear.

It's a textbook no-money-down real estate transaction that leaves everyone happy—JPMorgan, my daughters Leslie and Christina, Maggie, and me.

I'm sure my beloved Reginald is also pleased up in heaven as he watches his family finally secure a house he's coveted for years. I can practically see him grinning at me, as he says: "Loida! Go on with your baaaaad self!"

# 14

# FROM MRS. LEWIS TO MADAM CHAIR

Tomorrow is my first day at the helm of a company that generates more than $1.8 billion in annual revenues; has more than 4,500 total employees in France, Spain, Belgium, Norway, Germany, Ireland, Italy, and Thailand; and is hemorrhaging money like it's going out of style.

Does the prospect of diving headlong into this multinational pressure cooker frighten me? To be honest, no.

Do I find what I'm about to embark on to be intimidating as heck? Unquestionably!

However, I'm determined to revive the fortunes of a corporation I feel my husband gave his life for. Failure is not an option, but guiding the company's fortunes will take me away from my precious daughters, especially Christina, who I have re-enrolled in Manhattan's Dalton School, where she's taking middle-school courses.

Fortunately, Reginald's mom, Carolyn Fugett, is ever-ready to come from Baltimore and stay with Christina, should I need to be in Europe for two or three weeks. Leslie is already at Harvard College.

At this point, it is my sole responsibility to maintain the trajectory of my beloved's vision, which is to create intergenerational wealth for our family and our community.

The parliamentary procedures TLC Beatrice's corporate board uses to discuss, object to, amend, and pass motions can be found in a book titled *Robert's Rules of Order*, which I learned years ago as a University of the Philippines student government leader.

Growing up with an entrepreneurial father, a mother who worked tirelessly to organize the Catholic Women's League's initiatives in the Philippines, plus 24 years of marriage to Reginald, have given me a masterclass on motivating and inspiring people. This turns out to be useful for someone who will be leading everyone at TLC Beatrice International Holdings, from its board of directors down to rank-and-file employees.

My Christian values, including treating others as I wish to be treated, will guide how I deal with the corporation's executives, international managers, administrative staff, as well as shareholders and the media.

One of Reginald's favorite maxims was his desire to "maximize shareholder value." Along with further ingraining that into TLC Beatrice's ethos, I will make it a top priority to interact with employees and customers in a way that's consistently friendly, fair, and firm.

To fully maximize my communications skills, I need to chip away the thick Filipino accent I've had since arriving in the United States in 1968. To deal with that, I turn to Butch Meily, a fellow Filipino who performed masterfully as Reginald's director of communications and whom I've retained. Butch puts me in touch with Sam Chwat (pronounced "schwuh"), a speech therapist who's helped a bevy of well-known actors, as well as politicians, businesspeople, and diplomats to ditch, and acquire, accents.

A tall, sunny man who's heavyset and whose face is ringed by a closely cropped beard, Sam has a master's degree in speech pathology from Columbia University and runs the Sam Chwat Speech Center on West 16th Street in Manhattan. The walls of his office are lined with posters of Oscar- and Grammy-winning thespians, including Robert De Niro and Julia Roberts, who've benefitted from Sam's tutelage.

With Sam's help, over the course of two sessions a week for a month, I'm gradually able to turn "da," "dat," and "doze" into "the," "that," and "those."

Next: Butch turns his attention to the President's Report, a state-of-the-company document that he'll write and I'll read in front of TLC Beatrice's board of directors. With that in mind, we hire Patty Goodwin, who mentors public speakers and who has me read the President's Report from start to finish while she videotapes my delivery.

Once my remarks are in the can, Patty plays my video and critiques my speech as Butch and I listen. She lets about 60 seconds of videotape run and then suddenly pushes the pause button.

"The first glaring thing I'm noticing," she says, "is that you read without once looking up at your audience. That's a no-no!"

She restarts my video, lets it play a few more seconds, then turns it off in mid-sentence.

"Practice reading the speech several times, to the point of practically committing it to memory. Why? Because you should be looking at the audience, more so than looking at your prepared remarks. Only glance at the script to keep track of your progress, but never read it as if you're looking at it for the first time."

And so it goes, with me writing down pointers that will help TLC Beatrice's new chairwoman and chief executive officer (CEO) come off like a seasoned pro in the public-speaking arena.

Patty goes so far as to give me a mantra to repeat in my head whenever I'm approaching a podium or dais: "I am glad I am here. I am glad you are here. I care about you. I know that I know."

I'm instructed to always smile at my audience after being introduced. "They are eager to hear what you have to say. So, smile to indicate you are glad they are there to hear you. And that you care about them.

"Then, breath in. Breathe out. Breathe in. Breathe out. Begin."

Nothing is left to chance—I'm ordered to fold the upper-right corner on sheets of paper I'm reading from, so I can smoothly turn pages in front of my audience, instead of standing before them fumbling and bumbling. Or worse, accidentally grabbing two pages and going directly from page 1 to page 3.

I can't recall Reginald every receiving public-speaking instruction, making me wonder if he was a natural or quietly took a class without mentioning it? This isn't about competitiveness—if I can be half as mesmerizing as my beloved was in front of a microphone, I'll be delighted.

Breathe in. Breathe out. . . .

Not only would the next portion of my CEO makeover tickle Reginald to no end, I can hear him laughingly advising me, "You represent me!" It's time to dress for success, in a manner befitting the wife of Reginald F. Lewis, along with being the leader of TLC Beatrice International Holdings.

During the first year we were in Paris, Reginald bought me haute couture clothes he discovered in a Paris boutique, Eric Schiek, while on the way to his office on Rue Royal. The first time I tried the boutique's clothing, Reginald actually accompanied and had me model what he had selected. I loved the fact that, as busy as he was, Reginald took the time to see whether his picks looked good on me, along with ascertaining whether I liked them myself.

Now that I'm on my own, I don't have many haute couture dresses in my collection—too expensive! In terms of price and style, I'm more of a Talbot or Tahari woman, although I've strayed a few times by purchasing creations from Balenciaga, Chanel, and Giorgio Armani.

Now that I'm back in Manhattan, I have a hair stylist and makeup artist, Jorge Lopez, who I discovered in the Grace Saloon on West 58th Street, behind the Solow Building. Jorge's cryptic take on appearance is, "Without kindness, there is no style."

Now that I'm middle-aged, I'm finding that certain dietary practices can also work to the detriment of style! I love Filipino, Chinese, Japanese, Italian, Spanish, and French cuisine. Because rice seems to have an affinity for my midsection, I've directed two Filipina personal cooks that I hire, Gloria Josue and, beginning in 2000, Delia Juarez, to go easy on the rice. In time, I'll come to eliminate rice altogether.

One of the biggest changes to my lifestyle, as I'm preparing to lead TLC Beatrice International Holdings, has been on the spiritual plane. Along with staying close to God through prayer, I've started using the

Zen Buddhism technique to meditate. I've found that the stillness that's part of meditation, in conjunction with my habit of making daily journal entries, after reading *The Word Among Us* magazine, keeps me grounded. It also helps me spot short- and long-term priorities with greater ease.

When I officially take over the reins of TLC Beatrice International Holdings tomorrow, on March 29, 1994, I'm going to open the board meeting with a prayer for wisdom and discernment, which I'm sure will catch the board by surprise.

I figure since I am the chairwoman, I may as well do what comes naturally.

# 15

# LIQUIDITY CRISIS

The year 1993 is particularly calamitous for TLC Beatrice International Holdings, Inc. Not only does it lose a strong leader with the passing of Reginald, the company's chairman and chief executive officer (CEO), but 1993 sees Europe suffer its worst recession since World War II.

The leadup to Europe's brutal economic climate can be traced to the disintegration of the Soviet Union four years earlier, a new geopolitical reality that's a contributing factor to high unemployment and ballooning sovereign debts throughout Europe.

All of this occurs while Western Europe is conceiving the European Union, which begins with six member nations and grows to 12 by 1993. All of this impacts TLC Beatrice's businesses, which are primarily concentrated in Western Europe.

Further compounding this perfect storm of economic headwinds, the summer of 1993 dumps unseasonably heavy rains on Spain, Portugal, France, Italy, Germany, Belgium, Sweden, and Denmark, which are key ice cream markets for TLC Beatrice International

Holdings. As a result, net revenues associated with ice cream manufacturing and distribution drop a precipitous 50%.

Into this brutal financial environment comes TLC Beatrice's new chairman and CEO, Jean Fugett, Jr., Reginald's brother. After my husband learned of his brain cancer, he created an Office of the Chairman for his company and arranged for Jean to become vice chairman. In the event that Reginald's malady proved fatal, Reginald decreed that Jean was to become chairman and CEO.

I will always be grateful to my brother-in-law Jean. Even though he was devastated by his older brother's passing, Jean obeyed Reginald's wishes and dutifully took over TLC Beatrice International Holdings' top leadership post on January 19, 1993.

In the midst of grappling with his grief, Jean was immediately confronted by three crises that arise on his very first day at the helm.

Per Reginald's instructions, Jean travels to Washington, D.C., and meets with General Colin Powell to offer him the position of CEO. Sadly, the general is unwilling to accept because he has firm plans to disappear from public life at the end of President George H. W. Bush's administration. The inauguration of Bill Clinton is taking place the following day, January 20, 1993.

Soon after being turned away by Powell, Jean learns there's been an explosion at a TLC Beatrice ice cream factory located in Puerto Rico, which leaves the facility ablaze. It's not immediately clear if any injuries or deaths have resulted.

Jean's third bit of bad news has to do with a group of disgruntled TLC Beatrice shareholders. Formerly executives with now-defunct Drexel Burnham Lambert, the dissident shareholders have filed paperwork with the Securities and Exchange Commission in a bid to force TLC Beatrice to buy out their 25% stake in the company.

Again, all this is occurring on the same day Jean loses his loving, illustrious big brother.

When Jean shares Colin Powell's decision with me, we decide it's a good idea to retain the services of the Spencer Stewart Agency, a headhunting firm that can send us CEO candidates to interview.

I quickly notice that every prospect sent our way is a White male, with the exception of one Puerto Rican executive. While all of the would-be CEOs appear to be competent, they all covet what I consider to be excessive compensation.

None are willing to offer assurances they can return TLC Beatrice International Holdings to profitability, but all seemed to have gotten a memo stating that they need to promise to "do my best."

And if their best doesn't cut it and TLC Beatrice's fortunes can't be turned around, my beloved Reginald's life work would have been for nothing, and his estate would be severely devalued.

I don't care for how the CEO hunt is progressing, but finding chief executive officers isn't currently my top priority: Getting over Reginald's death, and filling the yawning chasm his departure has carved in my life, is.

My discombobulated, near-catatonic state doesn't begin to disappear until the fall of 1993. That's when I start holding weekly breakfast meetings with Jean at Harry Cipriani, an upscale Italian restaurant inside the Sherry Netherland Hotel, on 59th Street and Fifth Avenue in Manhattan.

It's beginning to dawn on me that TLC Beatrice International Holdings is floundering, as its total net income continues to dip, while its red ink is growing brighter.

On December 22, 1993, the company's board of directors is to meet at TLC Beatrice's corporate headquarters on the 48th floor of the famous Solow Building, located at 9 West 57th Street.

I wake up early that morning at 834 Fifth Avenue, and after praying, it becomes quite clear in my mind: "I should take over TLC Beatrice!" This epiphany fails to generate one iota of fear or trepidation within me.

I immediately walk from the master bedroom to Leslie's room, where's she's sleeping blissfully. She was elected a TLC Beatrice International Holdings board member at 18, a year before her father passed away, and is in town for today's board of directors meeting.

"Leslie, Leslie," I whisper, nudging my daughter's shoulder until her eyes finally flutter open. "I'm taking over the company!"

Still half asleep, Leslie blurts out: "Oh, Mom! What took you so long?"

She immediately sits up in her bed and begin strategizing as if channeling her father. "You should talk to Uncle Jean and Uncle Tony."

I head back to the master bedroom, which overlooks Central Park's 65th Street Children's Zoo, and tap out a number on the phone.

"Jean, I am ready to take over TLC Beatrice."

Following a moment or two of silence, Jean asks me, "When do you want to take over?"

"Today. At the board meeting."

"Why don't we elect you as chairwoman today and then at the shareholder's meeting in July, I'll resign as CEO?" I'm so glad he's making the transition smooth and uneventful, as opposed to arguing or trying to negotiate with me.

"Thank you, Jean. That's a great suggestion!"

Before hanging up, we preliminarily agree on a generous separation package for Jean, then I place a call to Reginald's other brother, Tony Fugett, who Jean nominated to sit on TLC Beatrice's board following Reginald's death. Tony listens attentively as I recount the conversation Jean and I just had.

Tony suggests that he, Jean, Leslie, and I present a united Lewis-Fugett family front, calling for the four of us to speak to the board members individually, ostensibly to bring them up to speed on our game plan.

The other people comprising TLC Beatrice International Holdings' brain trust are Lt. Col. Lee Archer, a business executive who was a Tuskegee Airman; Sam Peabody, a member of Manhattan's 400 High Society; Robert DeJongh, a renowned US Virgin Islands architect; James Obi, owner of a million-dollar equitable insurance agency in Manhattan; Charles Clarkson, Reginald's law partner; and Ricardo Olivares, a Californian businessman who was one of Reginald's main tennis partners when my soulmate traveled to Los Angeles.

Rounding out the board are Paul Biddleman and Frank Richardson, who are both with Carlton Investments and are spearheading the effort to force TLC Beatrice to register their 25% equity stake on the stock market so it can be sold.

I seriously doubt any of the other board members will object to me leading TLC Beatrice. The Lewis family owns 51% of the shares, plus the success or failure of the company will have a significant impact on our financial standing.

Anyway, thanks to my legal training, I know that if anybody objects to my bid to guide the company's fortunes, I can simply have him voted off the board during the July shareholders meeting.

So, when the board of directors for TLC Beatrice International Holdings, Inc., holds its 9 a.m. meeting on the 48th floor of the Solow Building on December 22, 1993, the board votes for me to become chairwoman, effective February 1, 1994. It's also resolved that the board will continue to have 12 members and Jean is to remain in the CEO slot until the board elects a new CEO during the annual shareholders meeting in July.

After all the procedural stuff is done and dusted, my ascension to chairwoman feels . . . natural. My sense is that the board has chosen the perfect person for the job because no one knows the company's intricacies better than I do and no one has more skin in the game than I do, as the widow of my beloved.

From my perspective, things are unfolding exactly as they should, in light of TLC Beatrice's money-losing travails. After the meeting ends, Jean invites everyone to join him at the Harvard Club, an invitation I accept. It's a foregone conclusion that we both love Reginald F. Lewis dearly and want more than anything to see TLC Beatrice realize its full potential.

When I go home after leaving the Harvard Club and gaze into my full-length bedroom mirror, the same Loida I've always seen stares back. I haven't magically grown four inches taller now that I'm about to be the chairwoman of a multinational corporation with nearly $2 billion in revenues. As I stand there, Isaiah 50:7 comes to mind: "Because the Lord God helps me, I shall not be dismayed. I have set my face like flint to do His will, and I know that I will triumph."

A few weeks later I step into a plush office on the 48th floor of 9 West 57th Street, overlooking snow-covered Central Park. I'm the chairwoman of TLC Beatrice International Holdings, but not the CEO yet. Time to get down to business.

I have asked for the corporation's top executives to meet me in a conference room directly beside the CEO's office. On one wall of the room hangs a framed painting of a smiling clown, created by French avant-garde painter Francis Picabia.

"What's the situation?" I ask a group that until this morning, simply regarded me as the spouse of the visionary financier who acquired TLC Beatrice for just under $1 billion in 1987. A dramatically different dynamic prevails now because I'm sitting at the head of a conference table as Reginald's successor. Chairwoman for the moment, I'll have CEO tacked onto my title in mere months.

The current CEO, Jean Fugett, isn't present. We'd agreed beforehand that I'll run this meeting, in order to get a feel for the company's top executives and their capabilities.

"The situation is, we have a liquidity problem," volunteers Al Fenster, executive vice president for finance and legal affairs. The other execs present, Kevin Wright, Dennis Jones, David Guarino, Charles Clarkson, and Carl Brody, bob their heads in agreement.

"What does that mean, exactly?" I respond. I'm not ashamed to ask questions, to let these men staring at me curiously know that they're privy to something I'm not. I checked my ego at the front door, right after coming through the main entrance on 57th Street. Whenever I'm unfamiliar with something, I'm instantly going to seek clarification.

"It means we do not have enough cash to meet payroll this month."

"How did that happen? Don't we own companies in Europe and Asia?" I ask incredulously.

"Yes, but last year wasn't a profitable one for our European subsidiaries," Al says.

"Well, how do we fix this? Does anyone have a suggestion?"

Dennis Jones, our executive vice president for operations who had worked with Beatrice International Foods for 17 years, catches my eye.

"We could borrow from our Irish potato chip company, Tayto. Its manager, Vincent O'Sullivan, has set aside several million dollars to buy land outside of Dublin."

Dennis adds that Tayto, which dominates most of the Irish potato-chip market, currently has its manufacturing operations within

Dublin's city limits. That scenario could open up TLC Beatrice to legal exposure should a fire or explosion at Tayto's plant harm or kill Dublin residents.

"Could someone get Vincent on the phone?" I ask.

Dennis Jones reaches for a telephone sitting atop the conference table and dials Vincent O'Sullivan in Dublin.

"Vincent, Mrs. Loida Lewis is now our corporate chairwoman," Dennis says into the telephone receiver. "She'd like to know whether TLC Beatrice can borrow from the bank account you've established to acquire land outside of Dublin?"

Because the phone lacks an intercom, no one else in the conference room can hear Vincent's reply as Dennis spends a couple of minutes listening attentively.

"Well, Vincent, Mrs. Lewis is here," Dennis finally says, pointing to the phone, then to me as he gestures as if to ask, "Do you want to speak with him?"

I nod, "Yes!"

"She'd like to speak to you," Dennis tells Vincent. "I'm putting her on now." Then Dennis slides the telephone across the conference table, so I won't have to reach for it.

"Good afternoon, Vincent," I say amiably. "I appreciate your willingness to consider extending a loan to TLC Beatrice International Holdings. We'll be able to pay it back with no problem. Dennis will discuss loan terms with you and can explain the liquidity crisis we're confronting here at the main office. I'm grateful for your cooperation!"

Vincent somewhat reluctantly agrees to talk to his bank about making a temporary loan for TLC Beatrice, a loan that will be guaranteed by Tayto's account.

After I hang up, Dennis explains Vincent was upset because he was on the verge of entering into a contract to purchase several acres of land outside Dublin that he'd had his eye on for years, for $30 million. I can empathize with that, but I know from experience that desirable real estate, just like "irresistible" artwork, comes and goes. My main concern is that it now appears we have addressed our liquidity problem for the time being.

"We could sell the company plane," suggests Carl Brody, someone Reginald often described as the best tax man in existence, bar none. "It costs $3 million a year to maintain."

"Who could best help us accomplish that?" I want to know.

"Captain Brendan Flannery," Dennis Jones chimes in. "As the captain of our plane, he knows the general aviation business backward and forward. He'd have no problem finding someone who might be interested in purchasing a pre-owned corporate jet."

"Dennis, please ask Brendan to start moving on that."

Every ear around the table perks up when I utter this. These executives all appreciate how much Reginald loved to travel in his "ultimate perk." The fact that I'm willing to put my beloved's plane on the chopping block shows I'm deadly serious about cutting costs at TLC Beatrice.

"Where else can we reduce expenses?" I ask, making eye contact with each executive arrayed around the conference table.

"We have two limousines that are under lease for the next three years. We could easily terminate those leases." Once again, Carl Brody pipes up with a common-sense approach to vanquishing our liquidity problem. I make a mental note to give extra weight to his cost-cutting proposals.

"Good suggestion. Who would take care of that?"

A tiny nod from Al Fenster indicates he's on the case. Along with the other ways it's benefitting me, this meeting should give me an excellent sense of who's wedded to old ways of doing things that aren't cost-effective in our current financial climate.

"What other pressing problems do we have?"

"The ice cream factory in Puerto Rico that blew up. An ammonia release killed an employee," Dennis notes quietly.

"Oh my God!"

Jean mentioned this to me earlier, but so much is bouncing around my brain that I had forgotten about the accident. We weren't aware at the time that a fatality had resulted.

"Who is taking care of this situation?"

"We closed down operations, and the manager in Puerto Rico is making arrangements to compensate the family of the deceased," Al Fenster notes.

"Please update me on those negotiations. See to it that compensation is fair and acceptable to the family. What's the insurance situation?"

At this point, about 20 minutes into the meeting, I've got a nice conversational give and take established with the top execs of TLC Beatrice International Holdings. I'm starting to feel comfortable, at ease. I suspected that's what would happen!

"We have filed a claim, and the insurance company's lawyers are in discussion with our lawyers," Al responds.

As I crisply ask questions and field answers, I know that before the week is out, I'll have to execute a plan that will deliver pain to the 48th floor of 9 West 57th Street.

Specifically, I need to reduce corporate staff by 50% because, with less revenue coming in, it doesn't make sense to sustain previous salary and benefit levels. Hopefully, I'm making a positive first impression in this conference room, but I know there's a good chance I may be referred to as dragon lady—or worse—before the week is out.

I really, really hate that I have to do this, but I would dislike it even more if TLC Beatrice wound up becoming insolvent.

As I begin the process of trimming corporate staff, I'm closely watching how people comport themselves around the office, including their interactions with subordinates and with supervisors. People tend to gravitate to those whose styles closely approximate their own, and I'm no different.

I prefer conciliation over confrontation, am pretty much egoless, and always try to cut to the chase rather than subject people to wordiness or bombast.

One of the first people I talk to is Al Fenster, whose leadership style is markedly different than mine. Reginald hired Al with an eye toward easing Jean's assimilation into TLC Beatrice. Over the course of our conversation, Al and I agree to a separation payment that's been stipulated in his employment contract.

Afterward, I'm delighted when Al informs me that the law firm where he was once a partner is more than happy to take him back.

I have a more painful conversation with Kevin Wright, because his father's company was Reginald's first corporate client. Also, like Reginald, Kevin is also Harvard Law grad, earning him the nickname

Reginald Lewis, Jr., around the office. Still, I have decided that he has to go. We finalize our talk by agreeing on terms for a separation settlement.

David Guarino was hired by Reginald to identify businesses for TLC Beatrice to acquire and operate. But that doesn't square with my goal of maximizing the company's value, then taking it public, or selling it. Expansion is no longer a big TLC Beatrice objective—creating wealth for shareholders is, with the majority owners being the Lewis family. So, I let David go also, with generous separation pay.

There's no way around the fact that I have to lay off most of the company's support staff. However, I see to it that Fay Jenkins and Norma Willis, who were with Reginald from the time he started his law firm on 99 Wall Street, are able to secure employment with Paul, Weiss, Rifkin, Wharton & Garrison, the Manhattan law firm Reginald joined after graduating from Harvard Law School.

I also release Diedre Wilson, who had been Reginald's personal assistant ever since he formed his own law firm. I'm relieved when Diedre informs me that she's going to use her separation pay to create a nursery/daycare and am thrilled she's making a foray into entrepreneurship.

The Reginald F. Lewis Foundation is housed in TLC Beatrice International Holdings' office space, but I'm going to downsize from the 32,000 square feet currently at our disposal, to a smaller 7,000-square-foot space. Therefore, I ask Foundation Vice President Beverly Cooper, who is Reginald's aunt, to move the foundation's documents from Manhattan to Baltimore. I also lay off the Reginald F. Lewis Foundation's secretary, Susan Washington.

After working with several temporary executive assistants, I find Lilly Black—who is single and very efficient—to permanently fill my EA slot.

Out of roughly 30 corporate staffers, I retain Dennis Jones, Carl Brody, Butch Meily, Terri Pike, and Bimal Amin. It's a painful process that had to be executed if TLC Beatrice International Holdings, Inc., is to survive.

In order for me to lead with maximum effectiveness, I need to be around people that I'm in sync with and that I can trust implicitly.

Someone who fits the bill beautifully is my sister Imelda "Mely" Nicolas, who I hire as special assistant to the chair.

After that, I go full circle by bringing aboard Rey Glover, who was my boss back in the days when I worked for the Law Students Civil Rights Research Council. I designate Rey TLC Beatrice's general counsel.

I also hire someone to be my chief financial officer, but his performance is so disastrous that I wind up firing him after only three months. But I get it right the second time by recruiting Peter Offermann, the Bankers Trust Company officer who loaned Reginald the bulk of the money needed to acquire the McCall Pattern Company.

At the end of the day, I end up very pleased with the makeup of my corporate staff and am ready to take on the world.

# 16

# PUTS AND CALLS

I've been TLC Beatrice's International Holdings' new chairwoman and CEO less than a year, and the positive impact of my tough-love leadership approach is starting to materialize on the company's balance sheet.

This seems to catch some industry observers by surprise. I'm not sure why, because what I've been doing is hardly rocket science: When a corporation is faltering financially and is at a point where it might not make payroll, it's time to cut fat. Period.

For the third quarter ending September 30, 1994, operational earnings are up by $5.5 million, or 18%, compared with the third quarter of 1993. Earnings per share for the third quarter of 1994 come in at $1, a 30% jump over the same period in 1993.

Year-to-date earnings per share for TLC Beatrice International are $1.68 on September 30, 1994, a 47% increase over the first three quarters of 1993. Among those who believed I could reinvigorate TLC Beatrice, and among those who felt I didn't have a snowball's chance of succeeding, no one can deny that the cost-reduction program I've put in place is starting to work.

To keep this positive trend going, I retain Chicago-based global management firm McKinsey & Co. to develop a long-range plan to maximize TLC Beatrice's European businesses. McKinsey is analyzing the sustainability of our competitive positions in each of the markets we're in, along with our prospects for growth and our capabilities for generating cash flow.

I'm starting to benefit from a mythology that's spreading throughout TLC Beatrice International Holdings: "Mrs. Lewis has an iron fist in a velvet glove!" I derive zero enjoyment from slicing expenses or laying off people, but my reputation does help keep employees motivated. So does TLC Beatrice's burgeoning financial performance, which is being aided by an economic climate in Europe that's starting to improve.

During my second year as chairwoman and CEO, overhead expenses are reduced from $20 million to $13 million in 1995, as net sales rise from $1.8 billion to $2 billion. During TLC Beatrice's board of directors meeting in Manhattan on April 28, 1995, the members of my board kindly note that I've been recognized by *Working Woman* as the magazine's top business woman of the year.

Obviously, I didn't take over the company looking for kudos and accolades. Still, it feels awesome to have my board acknowledge that TLC Beatrice's financial performance has improved under my guidance. And to be perfectly honest, the cover story *Working Woman* ran on me is gratifying. Plus, there's a good chance the positive publicity will come in handy at some point down the road.

Now that I'm getting into the swing of things, I've begun spending two weeks per month in Europe. It's good for the chairwoman and CEO to be walking factory floors, speaking with TLC Beatrice workers, and meeting managers. That imparts a much better sense of how the various components of my business are operating than studying balance sheets in Manhattan.

Mom comes to the rescue once more, because every time I leave New York, she stays with Christina in our Fifth Avenue duplex. It's family policy that, whenever possible, a relative stays with my youngest daughter when work takes me abroad.

Because Christina enjoys playing the piano, I find a topnotch Manhattan piano teacher to give her lessons. By the time my daughter turns 16, her skill level has reached a point where she's ready for a piano recital at Weill Recital Hall, which is part of Carnegie Hall. Thanks to Christina's focused regimen of practicing at least two hours a day, she performs magnificently during her recital, which I organized. Reginald would have been quite proud of Christina's performance.

However, not long after Carnegie Hall, Christina goes cold turkey on playing the piano, noting that "I'm not going to be a concert pianist. Too much time, too little money!" At her young age, she's already made a determination that music isn't her calling, and will eventually graduate from Harvard College cum laude with a bachelor's degree in liberal arts.

It pays to have a clear picture of what you find enthralling in life and what you consider drudgery.

For me, associating with malcontents is high on the list of things I don't particularly care for. But when two disgruntled shareholders pop up on my radar, I'm dutybound to make them one of my highest priorities.

Around the same time I take over TLC Beatrice International Holdings, a shareholder's suit is filed in Delaware against the company, the board of directors, Reginald's estate, and even Loida Nicolas Lewis! It irks me tremendously that the dissident shareholders, who are mostly former executives of defunct Drexel Burnham Lambert, didn't file their suit while my brother-in-law, Jean Fugett, Jr., was running the company.

I can't prove it, but I'd bet anything the shareholders have filed their legal action because a woman—me—is now in the driver's seat. This enrages me to no end because bald-faced sexism is at play here!

The lawsuit alleges that a five-year, $15-million compensation package for Reginald that the board approved on December 22, 1992, shouldn't have been paid to him. Ditto a $15-million sponsor fee that was eventually paid to Reginald after he acquired Beatrice International Foods on December 1, 1987. The lawsuit claims that the sums received by Mr. Lewis were actually dividends and should be returned to the company's treasury.

I recall how Reginald furiously contemplated walking away from the billion-dollar deal to buy Beatrice International Foods because he felt the firm that raised most of the money for his transaction—Drexel—made him jump through hoops to be paid sponsor fees that White corporate takeover artists routinely received upon closing their deals.

Thanks to the back and forth over my husband's compensation package, along with the quibbling over whether he deserved a sponsor fee for the Beatrice International deal, Reginald was never paid a cent during the five years he guided the fortunes of TLC Beatrice!

I direct Rey Glover to retain the most skilled trial lawyers he can find and have them oppose the shareholders' suit. This legal action is highly personal for me because I feel Reginald is being hectored and sullied beyond the grave, while I'm being forced to deal with a sexist double standard.

But as the individuals who filed the suit probably predicted, the litigation gets to be time-consuming as well as a drag on TLC Beatrice International Holdings' earnings. From a visceral standpoint, I feel like I could fight the shareholders' lawsuit forever. But when viewed through the lens of being a responsible, level-headed corporate leader, I see this legal action has become an exceedingly toxic distraction.

I know that emotions and business make terrible bedfellows, but I'm human! In light of who's behind this lawsuit, as well as its timing, I find it difficult to fight these allegations as though I'm an unfeeling automaton.

Ultimately, my tax expert, Carl Brody, says that because we paid federal income tax in 1993 on the $30 million approved by my board, if Reginald's estate returns his compensation to the company's coffers, Uncle Sam will return to his estate taxes paid in 1992.

I can live with this quid pro quo. I settle the litigation, ending something that had the potential to be a never-ending legal battle. Now, my focus can be solely on growing my late husband's corporation for the purpose of enhancing its value.

## COMING UP WITH $350 MILLION

While executing his leveraged buyout of Beatrice International Foods, Reginald took out a five-year, $350-million mezzanine loan from a

French bank operating under the aegis of the French government. Banque de Paris et des Pays-Bas, commonly referred to as Paribas, is an investment bank headquartered in Paris.

After the bank was subsequently privatized, Paribas somehow lost track of some of its debts, which are administered by a clerk and have very few administrative requirements! One day as the clerk is looking at balance sheets for loans worth $100 million and bigger that are to mature within a year's time, he comes across TLC Beatrice's $350 million loan.

When Paribas contacts us and finds we're making no effort to sell assets or otherwise raise capital so we can remove our $350 million obligation from Paribas' books, the bank freaks out. We do too because the loan instantly becomes a ticking time bomb. Even though Paribas dropped the ball in terms of keeping us apprised of the loan's status, the bank is free to call the loan if it wishes. That would have devastating consequences for TLC Beatrice International Holdings.

My team and I need to move heaven and earth to get rid of this $350 million debt, and we need to do it yesterday. Underscoring our urgency, Paribas lets us know in no uncertain terms that they want the loan retired.

My chief financial officer, Peter Offermann, reaches out to Paribas to see if they're willing to refinance the loan. They respond that they'll do half, $175 million, which they'll convert into long-term debt at terms that, naturally, are to Paribas' advantage. I reluctantly green light this. I have no choice because Paribas has TLC Beatrice between a rock and a hard place.

With $175 million still left to go, I direct Peter and Rey Glover, my general counsel, to start identifying underperforming, non-core TLC Beatrice International Holdings assets we can sell. Quickly.

We unload Choky, a French powdered drinks operation, and Premier Is A/S, a Norwegian ice cream manufacturer. We also sell TLC Beatrice's majority interest in Gelati Sanson S.p.A., an Italian ice cream unit, and divest ourselves of German ice cream manufacturer Artigel, which has a paltry single-digit share of its market.

Now that the Paribas conflagration has been extinguished, I begin concentrating on a relatively new French supermarket business named

Leader Price. The company was started in 1990 by brothers Jean and Jacques Baud (pronounced bow) and has grown so rapidly that by 1995 Leader Price has 250 stores throughout France. The concept behind Leader Price is simple: Fill its stores with private label Leader Price products whose quality is comparable to that of name brand goods but that sell at a lower price point.

The Baud brothers came upon the private label strategy through their ownership of Franprix, which along with Leader Price constitute the two largest grocery store chains in France. When the Bauds first tried out the private-label idea at Franprix, items flew off the shelves. Afterward TLC Beatrice International Holdings, under Reginald's direction, cannily entered into a partnership where TLC Beatrice invested $3 million to help build Leader Price stores.

Toward the end of 1995, Peter Offermann warns me of an impending TLC Beatrice financial conundrum: In 1990, TLC Beatrice entered into an agreement to own 51% of Leader Price, with the Bauds holding 49%. Woven into the deal is a stipulation that when 1997 arrives, TLC Beatrice can buy out the Bauds' 49% for a price equal to 13 times Leader Price's annual cash flow.

But the pact also gives the Bauds' the option of compelling TLC Beatrice to purchase that 49% at a multiple of 15 times cash flow in 1997. This arrangement between TLC Beatrice and the Bauds is known as a *put and call option*.

Peter explains that because Leader Price is currently generating huge amounts of cash flow, if we wait until 1997 and then the Bauds suddenly activate their clause, our financial obligation to buy them out could easily be $100 million more than it currently is.

To get rid of this sword of Damocles dangling over our heads, it's imperative that we persuade the Bauds to push the triggering deadline out another five years, making it 2002 instead of 1997.

Achieving an expanded timeline will likely prove to be an interesting negotiating challenge. In addition to being highly skilled businessmen, the Bauds have prickly personalities that make them exceedingly difficult to work with.

In December 1995, I travel to the office of Jean Baud, a tall, good-looking man who has a full head of grey hair, along with a Gaelic air of self-confidence that borders on arrogance. Accompanied by the top executive of TLC France, Daniel Jux, I personally present Jean with a $20,000-Patek Philippe watch as a gift for his 75th birthday. Through Daniel, who's serving as my interpreter, I let Jean Baud know of my desire to sit down with him soon so that we can discuss the possibility of pushing our put and call deadline out to 2002.

Daniel is still in Jean Baud's office when I depart, feeling optimistic that I've managed to convince Jean to extend the put and call deadline by five years. However, when a grim-faced Daniel enters my Paris office on Rue Royale later, I'm crushed. Seems Jean Baud declared that an extension is out of the question.

Jean Baud's behavior is somewhat puzzling because it's hardly as though he's dealing from a position of strength. When Reginald acquired Beatrice International Foods, it already held a 93% stake in Franprix! Then my beloved negotiated a majority 51% ownership position in Leader Price when he provided the Bauds with $3 million to get Leader Price started.

The Bauds are primarily talented operators of France's two largest grocery stores, but the majority owner of both entities is me!

Following Jean Baud's disappointing decision, Peter Offermann, Rey Glover, and I spend a good part of 1996 mapping out our next move. Thanks to a law France has passed that prohibits foreign grocery chains such as Walmart or Aldi from doing business in the country, the value of French supermarket companies is sky high.

Carrefour, a French multinational corporation that operates hypermarkets, grocery stores, and convenience stores throughout France, has a stock price that's 37 times cash flow. Because TLC Beatrice's put is 13 times Leader Price's cash flow, while the call held by Leader Price is 15 times its cash flow, TLC Beatrice should be able to sell our majority shares in Leader Price for far more than 15 times cash flow.

Using Carrefour as a guidepost, TLC Beatrice could possibly even receive 37 times Leader Price's cash flow. With that in mind, I give the okay for investment bankers to seek potential buyers for the Leader Price and Franprix equity held by TLC Beatrice.

Within a few days, French supermarket chain Casino makes a $597-million bid for TLC Beatrice's shares of Leader Price and Franprix. We close the deal on August 30, 1997.

Using cash from the Leader Price/Franprix sale, we pay off the $175 million that TLC owes French bank Paribas, meaning that TLC Beatrice International Holdings, Inc., is now debt-free!

With excess cash on our books, we decide to pay small dividends to our shareholders but are aware that paying dividends isn't a tax-efficient course of action. Dividends are considered income and are taxed at a 39% rate for high-net-worth individuals under the US tax code. But if we liquidate the company, the tax rate on capital gains is only 20%.

It's clear to me that the time has come to liquidate TLC Beatrice International Holdings, Inc. As I arrive at this decision, I recall something my beloved had a habit of repeating over and over: "The goal is to create wealth, not build an empire!"

# 17

# WINDING DOWN TLC BEATRICE

**P**rior to TLC Beatrice International Holdings, I'd never run a multibillion-dollar, multinational corporation. Now, I'm about to liquidate one.

Thousands of tomes have been written about creating successful businesses, but no one has published a how-to focusing on intentionally dismantling one. That's alright, because I've got the brainpower of Chief Financial Officer Peter Offermann and General Counsel Rey Glover, along with the experience of having already sold a French grocery-store monopoly valued at more than half a billion dollars.

Thusly armed, I sit down with Peter and Rey during fall 1997, and we discuss the best way to propel TLC Beatrice along the road to dissolution. Is selling what's left of the company in one big chunk the best way to create value? Or should we embrace a strategy of gradually breaking the corporation into pieces?

Our consensus is that selling TLC Beatrice one component at a time is the way to go. Obviously, this will take longer than having a buyer swoop in and write a single check for what remains of my beloved's acquisition. But the priority here is to get the most we can for the company as opposed to rushing helter-skelter through the liquidation process.

In July 1998, I give Peter and Rey the okay to retain Goldman, Sachs & Co. to oversee the sale of what's left of TLC Beatrice. The focus initially falls on a Spanish ice cream business we have a 65% stake in—Helados La Menorquina, in Barcelona, and Kalise, in the Canary Islands.

Our partner in Spain is tennis-playing Delfin Suarez, 65, who founded the ice cream units we're looking to divest.

Multinational corporations Nestlé and Unilever are quick to express an interest in buying the Spanish operations, but Nestlé drops out of the negotiations early on, citing an unspecified antitrust concern. This isn't a problem because TLC Beatrice is most interested in Unilever: We feel the deal would dovetail nicely with their strategic interests.

Unfortunately, it quickly becomes apparent from Unilever's posturing that they feel they're our best prospect. They toss out a less-than-head-turning bid, and when we subsequently meet with them in London and suggest a more realistic price, Unilever's representatives walk out of the meeting!

The Iberian Beverage Group of Spain ultimately wins the right to TLC Beatrice's stake in the Spanish ice cream business for $191 million.

When Reginald acquired Beatrice International Foods in 1987, he and Delfin Suarez signed a contract that gave Delfin the right to match the terms and conditions of the winning bidder, if TLC Beatrice ever sold its equity in Delfin's business.

After the Iberian Beverage Group of Spain moves in, Delfin decides to exercise his right of first refusal and gets Spanish banks to finance his matching bid. This enables him to achieve 100% ownership of the ice cream manufacturing plants he created in Barcelona and the Canary Islands.

TLC Beatrice exits Spain.

Next up is Tayto, the Irish potato chip company. Our manager there, Vincent O'Sullivan, has been an exemplary performer and has retained Merrill Lynch as his investment banker in a bid to buy the company.

Vincent is up against Cantrell & Cochrane Ltd., an Irish beverage company.

To make sure the bidding process remains impartial, I establish a Chinese wall that will facilitate the highest bidder winning Tayto, although my personal preference is definitely for Vincent to win the company he's served with distinction.

However, when the bidding starts, Vincent and Merrill Lynch come up $1 million short. Vincent loses out, and the company where he's worked diligently for years is sold to Cantrell & Cochrane for $116.5 million.

Both Vincent and I are crushed.

In light of how things turn out, I distribute $1 million among Tayto's 350-person workforce, to thank them for their hard work over the years. The payouts are based on seniority, meaning that employees who've been with Tayto since it opened its doors 35 years ago will receive the most money.

Exit Ireland.

Talented second-generation entrepreneur Jacques Heyman's runs Sunco, a Belgium company that produces soft drinks and mineral water bottled in Belgium, the Netherlands, and St Albans, France. Most of what Sunco makes is sold by supermarket chains as private-label brands.

In June 1998, we sell our stake in Sunco and two other bottling companies for $44 million, erasing TLC Beatrice's footprint in Belgium, the Netherlands, and St. Albans, France.

A Thai soft drink company, Bireley's, is the last subsidiary TLC Beatrice holds equity in. This firm is so tiny that my team never visits it; doing so would meaningfully impact Bireley's profits! The orange-flavored drink the company produces has a minuscule market share compared with Thailand's leading soft drink brand.

In 2000, Bireley's managing partner Mark Whitfield and his family buy the company from TLC Beatrice.

Exit Thailand.

TLC Beatrice decided to export the Franprix supermarket concept to China as part of an initiative spearheaded by my sister, Mely Nicolas, and her business partner, Dan Oñate. I personally loaned them money that enabled them to buy TLC Beatrice China, including a total of 50 stores in Xiamen and Chengdu.

Exit China.

With that last sale, TLC Beatrice International Holdings, Inc., one of the most improbable business entities of all time, no longer exists. But significantly, before it closes its doors, TLC Beatrice successfully creates wealth, which is why my husband created it. When Reginald passed away in 1993, a share of TLC Beatrice International Holdings, Inc., was worth $20. When TLC Beatrice is totally liquidated in 2000, shares of the company are valued at $50, CFO Peter Offermann affirms.

Reginald, yours truly helped put the finishing touches on what you set out to accomplish, my beloved—wealth generation!

## You Can't Win Them All

Toward the beginning of 2000, I'm feeling pretty pleased with myself after the shareholders of TLC Beatrice International Holdings receive healthy financial distributions stemming from their investment in the corporation.

One of TLC Beatrice's biggest shareholders is former Drexel Burnham Lambert partner, Mike Milken, who was Reginald's main financial banker for the purchase of Beatrice International Foods. When Leslie and I find ourselves visiting Los Angeles, Michael graciously takes us out to dinner. Another satisfied investor sends me a bottle of Dom Perignon champagne, while yet another sends a bouquet of flowers.

My TLC Beatrice track record prompts the *New York Times* to publish a long story on my reign as chairwoman and CEO. Bloomberg TV, the Charlie Rose Show, and the *Wall Street Journal* wind up doing profiles on me and my business success.

In the Philippines, all of the major newspapers and magazines run pieces about how my corporate achievements are unrivaled when it comes to Filipino emigrants who've gravitated to the United States.

There's so much acclaim and hoopla associated with my name that I conveniently forget the timeless advice of Proverbs 16:18—*Pride goeth before destruction.*

I also forget what Reginald continually drilled into the heads of would-be entrepreneurs who approached him for business advice: "Buy an existing business. DO NOT start a business! Ninety percent of start-ups fail. Why would you bet on the 10% chance that you would succeed?"

Having enjoyed tremendous success during my seven-year run at TLC Beatrice International Holdings, I'm looking to replicate that success as Rey Glover and I spend $800,000 to acquire LionHeart, a Florida company that supplies supermarkets and wholesale businesses with fresh fruits and vegetables.

Feeling unduly confident following my performance at TLC Beatrice, with LionHeart I overlook one of the cardinal rules of investing in, or running, a startup business: You need to keep a watchful eye on things 24 hours a day, seven days a week, without exception. I've been spoiled by working in concert with the top-notch managers of companies such as Franprix, Tayto, etc.

They were on top of every facet of their businesses, enabling me to shift my focus to other priorities. I'm still locked into my TLC Beatrice mode of thinking, so I let my LionHeart partners in Florida do their thing, while I address other matters.

The result? US Bankruptcy Court after five years.

Because I have international business experience, I take over the management of Beatrice China and dismiss the firm's managing partners, my sister Mely Nicolas and Danny Oñate, who are responsible for getting Beatrice China up and running.

Afterward, I foolishly turn down a $30-million buyout offer from a Singapore supermarket company that wants to purchase the 150 convenience stores Dan and Mely have built in Xiamen, Suzhou, Beijing, Chengdu, and Guangzhou. I reject the buyout because a $3-million loan I extended to Beatrice China wouldn't be paid at closing but three years afterward.

As a result, the Singapore firm buys a different convenience store chain operating in China. My company, Beatrice China, can't keep up with the local competition, which is being backed by the Chinese government. If we build 10 new convenience stores, it seems our competitors have already constructed 100 stores, thanks to financing from China's state-controlled banks.

Bankruptcy after seven years.

When I launch Beatrice China, which takes place after the dissolution of TLC Beatrice, I also create Beatrice Philippines. I construct a Philippine slaughterhouse in Naga, with the goal of helping local pig farmers in the Bicol Region of the Philippines, where I grew up. However, our partners are using Beatrice Philippines trucks to transport pork products from our slaughterhouse to Manila and are then funneling the payments they receive into their personal bank accounts.

Result? Bankruptcy after seven years.

What did I learn from these three business fiascos? That I no longer have the energy, or patience, to invest in startup businesses and then do the work and handholding needed to make them viable.

Three very painful lessons that cost me dearly. But at least I stop making major investments in fledgling business enterprises.

## MATTERS OF THE HEART

*"I've been married to a king. . . ."*

"How come you never remarried after Reginald passed away?" That question has been lobbed at me more times than I can count.

Well, my thinking has always been that I'll never encounter anyone who can measure up to my beloved. So, why bother to look? But just because you aren't actively searching, that doesn't mean someone won't come along and tweak your heart strings when you least suspect it.

This happens to me at least twice in the time since my husband left this earth on January 19, 1993.

As I'm running TLC Beatrice, I travel to the Philippines and run into the widower of a woman who was a law school classmate when I was at the University of the Philippines. Reginald knew her husband, who was a politician, because when the couple visited New York, we invited them to dinner.

In the back of my mind, I'm thinking that nothing will come of my encounter with the politician. That's because he's seeking someone like my classmate, meaning a woman who will make sure all his needs are taken care of.

Still, I date the politician in the Philippines, but never alone. He invites me out, but dating in the Philippines is always done as a group. I've always found this man attractive, even when I was a law student. I contemplate being with him one-on-one, and tell him that if he ever visits New York, he can feel free to call me.

But when he does come to New York, he's in another relationship. In a way I'm relieved because, although I'm tempted, I choose to remain in New York with my daughters and successfully run TLC Beatrice.

The other man who piques my interest is a New Yorker, a well-to-do executive who happens to be in the leveraged buyout business. He's married and in the process of divorcing, which I'm not aware of at the time.

He's handsome, a central casting White Anglo-Saxon Protestant who attended Harvard Law School, one year ahead of Reginald, and he's a member of my board. My close friends know I'm attracted to him.

I never go on a date with him because once you do that, it's implied that you like the person, which leads to this and that. I asked myself: "How will I date a married man, when I know that I don't want to be part of a marriage breakup?" So, no-go.

Another friend calls me to say, "So and so is interested in you. Are you dating?" I tell her no—not available! I have two girls who are still with me, one's in college and the other's in middle school. Those are two full-time jobs, plus I have a business to run!

My sense is that dealing with this man will prove to be more of a distraction than anything.

Reginald is my only love, the man I had a full life with during our nearly 25 years together. Robert Browning's poem comes to mind, "How do I love thee? Let me count the ways. . . ."

When my soulmate dies, it's an event that leaves me totally distraught and discombobulated. But my faith in a loving God keeps me steady, because in my heart I know God will not abandon me, God will not leave me an orphan. He will not let go of me.

Every morning when I get up, there's no loneliness. I wanted to be a nun earlier in life, and in an odd way I am one, faithful to prayer and leading a life of service.

In 1999, I start taking a management class at Harvard Business School, and one of my classmates is very, very direct: "I'm going to marry you, and we're going to get married at St. Patrick's Cathedral!"

He's a WASP, handsome, a little overweight, and has a very successful ice cream franchise.

He also has a great sense of humor and is great company, but I'm at a point in my life where I've decided that I honestly don't want any emotional or romantic entanglements.

I didn't enter the management class looking for romance; I enrolled to earn a Harvard certificate, since my beloved husband, both daughters, and two sons-in-law all have Harvard diplomas.

Yes, I'm competitive!

I'm still good friends with all three of those men and send them Valentine's Day cards every year. The relationships are platonic, but they are still dear to me.

But it goes without saying that I'm eternally grateful to God for putting Reginald and me together, according to His purpose.

# 18

# PROGENY, PHILANTHROPY, POLITICS

I turned 80 (gulp) on December 23, 2022.

In all seriousness, that number only signifies that I've had more time than most to cherish victories, learn from miscues and failures, and identify avenues likely to inspire and motivate others.

Following an existence where business and the law were major factors in my life, these days my adult children, my grandchildren, philanthropy, and politics are where I'm putting the bulk of my focus.

Tall, handsome Christian, 17, is level-headed and wise beyond his years, while his lovely sister Savilla, 17, has an inquisitive mind that catalogs world capitals with ease. When they were less than a year old, Christian and Savilla were brought to the United States from Rwanda by my daughter, Leslie, and her then-husband, Gavin Sword.

Christina and her spouse, Daniel Halpern, have blessed me with dutiful, compassionate Calvin, 11, and with Sasha, a 8-year-old who has an artistic bent and a knack for forging friendships. Rounding out my grandchildren is little Macy, who's very active and surprisingly articulate for someone not yet 3.

Along with monitoring the positive trajectories of my grandkids, something else I derive tremendous pleasure from is my daughters' fierce embrace of altruism and activism.

Leslie has co-founded MultiGenerational.Black a financial services company seeking to alleviate the United States' racial wealth gap, while Christina is leading our family's efforts to have a feature film made about Reginald, based on his bio, *Why Should White Guys Have All the Fun?*

I am very proud and appreciative of my brilliant, socially conscious, beautiful women!

On the philanthropic front, I'm the chairwoman of the Reginald F. Lewis Foundation, which my beloved Reginald incorporated in 1987. Other members of the board of directors include my daughter, Christina, my brother-in-law, Tony Fugett, and the youngest of Reginald's aunts, Beverly Cooper. Leslie, who is now a director emeritus, was appointed to the board by her father when she turned 18.

In keeping with a $3-million pledge Reginald had made to his alma mater, Harvard Law School, my daughters and I met with Dean Robert Clark in April 1993 to unveil the Reginald F. Lewis International Law Center. It marked the first time an Ivy League school named one of its buildings after an African American.

After I became the foundation's chairwoman, $5 million was donated toward the construction of the Reginald F. Lewis Museum of Maryland African American History & Culture, in Baltimore, followed by more than $1 million for The Lewis College (TLC), a school in Sorsogon, Philippines, that's named after my late husband. His undergraduate alma mater, Virginia State University, named its business school after Reginald a few years ago, following a $1.5-million donation from the foundation.

The foundation recently pledged $5 million toward the creation of the Obama Presidential Center, which will be the Chicago-based presidential library of former President Barack Obama and is slated to have a Reginald F. Lewis meeting room.

When it comes to politics, around the time that I was liquidating TLC Beatrice International Holdings, I was becoming more politically active in the United States and in the Philippines. Working with Alex Esclamado, Rodel Rodis, Michael Dadap, and Gloria Caoile, I formed the National Federation of Filipino American Associations, which celebrated 25 years of existence in 2022.

I vigorously supported Hillary Clinton in 1999 when she ran for her US Senate seat in New York and joined the campaign of Barack Obama after he won the Democratic presidential nomination in 2008 and again in 2012.

During the 2010 Philippine presidential election, a group that I belonged to—US Pinoys for Noy-Mar—campaigned hard and won, paving the way for six years of impressive Philippine economic expansion.

Thank God Joe Biden won the US Presidency in 2020! To help his cause, I campaigned with the Asian American Pacific Islander (AAPI) Victory Fund, chaired by Indian American Shekar Narasimhan.

In 2022, I was involved in the Philippines presidential campaign of Leni Robredo, who lost to Ferdinand "Bongbong" Marcos after being subjected to a massive social media disinformation campaign.

As someone who's been a New Yorker the past 50 years, I enthusiastically campaigned for Steven Raga, who was elected in November 2022 as the first Filipino American to win a seat in the New York State Assembly!

In many ways, my life is the same now as when I was in my 60s, 40s, and 20s. My routine is packed with activities and causes that I fervently believe will benefit the Lewis family, our society, and the world.

### Insights

I don't profess to having unraveled the mystery of life, but I have glommed onto some valuable nuggets of wisdom over the years.

First: women can be effective leaders without emulating the negative behaviors often exhibited by powerful men. By that, I mean being unduly harsh with subordinates or continually unleashing salty, four-letter epithets. Instead, I found that firmness, fairness, and unassailable competence effectively shut down the second-guessers and naysayers.

Second: when setting goals in life, be flexible. I was supposed to have been either a nun or a public servant, which would include becoming a member of the Philippine Senate. Falling in love was the furthest thing from my mind, then along came Reginald F. Lewis!

Third: try to always be full of joy and gratitude. Our frame of mind determines whether we see the world in darkness or in light. Being a born-again Catholic, I'm constantly asking myself—when I speak or act, does it bring joy? If the answer is negative, that's a good time to reflect on what needs to be said or done.

Fourth: listen to your body. Pushing myself too hard and too fast and generally acting as if I were Superwoman contributed to me becoming ill with tuberculosis. The Greeks had it right—it's all about moderation!

Fifth: everything will be all right in the end. If it is not all right, it is not the end. Life happens.

As I've made clear throughout this book, spirituality is at the core of my being. My faith has played an integral role in my journey through life, so I'd like to bring things to a close with Psalm 3:5–6, my favorite:

> *Trust in the Lord with all your heart.*
> *Do not depend on your own understanding.*
> *Seek His will in all you do,*
>
> *And He will show you which path to take.*

# 19

# PHOTO GALLERY

1948. My mother's parents and siblings
From left to right (children): (Baby) Cecilia Mañalac, Eduardo Mañalac, Imelda Nicolas, Danilo Nicolas, Loida Nicolas, Jose Nicolas.
Seated from left to right: Virginia (Valenzuela) Mañalac, Magdalena (Mañalac) Nicolas, Grandma Asuncion (Enriquez) Mañalac, Grandpa Roman Mañalac, Purita Manalac, Luz Mañalac. Standing from left to right: Pedro Mañalac, Francisco de Jesus Nicolas, Mency Mañalac, Francisco Mañalac, Manuel Mañalac.

1953. The Nicolas Family. Seated from left to right: Francisco Jr. Magdalena (nee Mañalac), Francisco Sr. Standing from left to right: Imelda, Jose, Danilo, and Loida 11 years old.

1955. St Agnes Academy in Legaspi, Philippines, with the German Benedictine nuns (Sister Anunciata, Mother Superior Godfrieda, Sister Pudentiana) who ingrained into our psyche *Ora et Labora*, which means "Pray and Work." Imelda seated third from left. Loida standing second from left
*Source*: Leonor Cabigao-Bismonte.

1959. Physics class at St. Agnes Academy.
Seated from left is Bernarda Lita; standing are Edna C. Triunfante, Sr. Liboria, our physics instructress, Leonor Cabigao, Loida M. Nicolas, and Erlinda Gonzales.
*Source*: Leonor Cabigao-Bismonte

1969. Loida's and Reginald's wedding in Manila Philippines. From left to right: children Roman Gardose, Carolyn Corleto, Asunción Manalac, Danilo Nicolas II.
Standing from left to right: (Mama) Magdalena Nicolas, Imelda Nicolas, Loida, Reginald, (Papa) Francisco Nicolas Sr., Francisco Nicolas Jr., Jose Nicolas, Danilo Nicolas.

1972. Loida published *Ningas-Cogon* (brush-fire), an anti-martial law news magazine until 1979. Well-known cartoonist Nonoy Marcelo depicts a newly arrived Filipino in front of the iconic Flatiron Building, in Manhattan's Flatiron District.

(By artist James Gayles, 1978) Reginald told Loida that this drawing, which he hung in his study, accurately depicts what being Black in America feels like.

1988. Leslie, Reginald, Christina, and Loida in our 25-room apartment in Place du Palais Bourbon Paris where we lived until 1993.

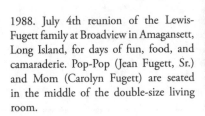

1988. July 4th reunion of the Lewis-Fugett family at Broadview in Amagansett, Long Island, for days of fun, food, and camaraderie. Pop-Pop (Jean Fugett, Sr.) and Mom (Carolyn Fugett) are seated in the middle of the double-size living room.

1989. Loida and Reginald on the lawn of Broadview, having just renewed their marriage vows on their 20th anniversary.

1989. Carolyn, and Reginald chuckle as Loida recounts how she told her future husband "I don't want to see you anymore!" prior to proposing to him. The three are at Broadview, in Amagansett, Long Island, to mark Loida's and Reginald's 20th anniversary.
*Source*: Maria Mañalac Capati

1989. Photographed at Amagansett, Long Island, Labrador retrievers Gaston and Gilbert accompanied Loida, Reginald, and Christina from Paris to New York every summer.

1998. Serving as Grand Marshall of the Centennial Celebration of Philippine Independence Day, Loida waves a Philippine flag while marching down Madison Avenue in Manhattan.
First row from left to right: Imelda "Mely" Nicolas and Carolyn "Mom" Fugett.
Second row from left to right: Asunción "Chong" Mañalac-Capati, Suzzette Bagaybagayan Rutherford, (partly hidden) Mency Mañalac-Gardose.
*Source*: Irving Spivey

1992. Reginald looks on proudly as Loida signs a copy of her book, *How to Get a Green Card*, during a book launch inside the United Nations complex in Manhattan.

1994. The dedication of the Reginald F. Lewis International Law Center on Harvard Law School's campus, Cambridge, Massachusetts.
*Source*: Harvard Law School

1994. *New York Times* coverage of Loida taking control of TLC Beatrice as chairwoman and CEO.

1994. Loida exiting the luxurious TLC Beatrice corporate jet she would eventually sell to reduce the company's expenses. This shot was taken during a trip to Dublin to visit a TLC Beatrice operating unit. Behind Loida is Rene "Butch" Meily, who adroitly managed TLC Beatrice's corporate communications.

1996. TLC Beatrice's board of directors. Seated from left to right: Samuel Peabody, Leslie Lewis, Loida Lewis, Lee Archer. Standing from left to right: Clifford Alexander, Reynaldo Glover, Anthony Fugett, Robert DeJongh, William Webster, Ricardo Olivares, James Obi.

Loida donated the portrait of Reginald F. Lewis, which was painted by Hughie Lee-Smith, to the Harvard Club of New York City. *Source*: Lee White

1999. Loida, right, and event speaker First Lady Hillary Clinton at a National Federation of Filipino American Associations (NaFFAA) conference in Manhattan.

2005. The opening of the Reginald F. Lewis Museum of Maryland African American History & Culture, in Baltimore. Left to right are Leslie, Mom Carolyn Fugett, Loida, and Christina.

2008. Loida and presidential candidate Barack Obama in Manhattan. Obama was a student at Harvard Law School in 1990, the year Reginald Lewis decided to donate $3 million to the institution.

2008. Loida during an event commemorating the 100th anniversary of the University of the Philippines' founding in 1908. A 1967 graduate of the university's law school, Loida was honored with a Most Outstanding Global Alumna award.

2010. Christina, Loida and Leslie during a fundraising gala held at their "Daddy Warbucks" home in East Hampton, Long Island

2020. Loida and Joe Biden in Las Vegas, where Loida's campaign work with the Asian American Pacific Islander Victory Fund helped Biden to secure the White House. AAPI's vote helped him win the primary in Nevada and eventually led to his winning the presidency.

2010. Philippines President Benigno Aquino III, whose political ascendancy was aided by Loida's campaign work with the US Pinoys for Noynoy-Mar political organization.

2022. The Lewis-Sword-Halpern family. First row from left to right: Calvin Lewis Halpern, Savilla Lewis Sword, Loida, Sasha Lewis Halpern Macy Lewis Halpern. Pet Amber in front.
Standing from left to right: Dan Halpern, Christina Lewis, Christian Lewis Sword, Leslie Lewis.
*Source*: Enrico Dungca

The Lewis College, in Sorsogon, Philippines. Since 2000, Reginald F. Lewis' exhortation to "Keep going, no matter what!" has inspired students to attempt to realize their biggest dreams.

1990. In their Paris apartment, Leslie asked Loida and Reginald to make funny faces, prior to posing for a more formal shot.
*Source*: Leslie Lewis

*Source*: Photo by Sonny Austria/The Filipino Express

# ACKNOWLEDGMENTS

First and foremost, thanks be to God that Blair S. Walker and I have been able to confer, write, edit, and finish this manuscript on time.

I will always be grateful to Gerry Gil. In June 1968, Mely and I visited him at Stanford University, after flying from New York City on our way to the Philippines. After seeing how dejected I was, because I left my sweetheart in NYC and had no intention of returning, Gerry uttered three words: "Just call him!" I did, and tearfully told Reginald I was coming back. So, thank you, Gerry. Were it not for your advice, the story in the book would not be.

Thank you to my team at John Wiley & Sons; Copyeditors Kim Wimpsett and Sheryl Nelson; Editorial Assistant Jozette Moses; Content Specialist Jayalakshmi Et; Senior Marketing Manager Jeanenne Ray; and Senior Managing Editor Michelle Hacker. Special thanks to Andrew Tien, a former John Wiley & Sons employee who helped me find a home for my book at Wiley.

As I cruised down memory lane to pen my autobiography, I was aided by my sister, Imelda (Mely) Nicolas, who provided sorely needed roadmaps, as did Angie Cruz, Josefina Opeña Disterhoft, TLC executives Peter Offermann, Rene (Butch) Meily, and the excellent minutes Charles Clarkson created during TLC Beatrice board meetings.

Thank you to my loyal, long-term officemates, who are always ready to support my endeavors: my Executive Assistant Lilly Black and my Chief Financial Officer Bimal Amin.

Kudos to my personal staff that helps keep me healthy and on top of my game: Délia Juarez, Alice Balbuena and Lucien Stoutt. Previously, Stella Ylagan, Gloria Josue, Halette Douglas, Dalma Walker and Isola Williams. In Manila, my cousin Grace Enriquez, Charmane Calamiong, Fe Chico, Richard Alcobendas, Raul Dado. Previously, Liza Soriano.

In Paris, Patrick Lelong, who recently retired after 35 years and was replaced by his son Victor Lelong, and *gardienne* Manuela Rodrígues.

For helping me secure many of the photos displayed in this book, I tip my hat to; Lee White, Lora Nicolas Olaes, Enrico Dungca, Sonny Austria, Leonore Cabigao Bismonte, Irving Spivey, Chong Capiti, Elliott Wiley Sr., Bituin and Arnold Aquino, who are also my webmasters and directors of communications. who are also my webmasters and directors of communications duo.

For their support, my classmates from St. Agnes Academy: Rocio Casimiro Nuyda, Leonore Cabigao Bismonte, Norma Balana Rubio, Salvacion (Sonty) Lee, Jennie Yap Chan, Filipinas (Babie) Lianko Chua, and my loyal friends in the United States: Isabel Reyes Juan, Marilyn Crawford, Potri Ranka Manis, Cheryl McNeil, Celia Lamkin, and Jane Fields, Jose Ramos, Eric Lachica, Aida Bartolome, Edwin Josie, Jerry Sibal, Nanding Mendez, Nilsa Santiago, Bruce Cohen, and many more.

Love and warm regards go out to my Baltimore siblings, wonderful Jean, Anthony, Rosalyn, Joseph, and Sharon of the Fugett family, Reginald's brothers and sisters. And, of course, his formidable mother who has become Mom to me, also, Carolyn Fugett.

When speaking truth to power, it's helpful to be in the company of stalwart, courageous allies. Folks like Celia Lamkin, Rocio Nuyda, Eduardo Manalac, Eric Lachica and Rodel Rodis, who along with several other Filipino Americans joined me in filing a lawsuit against Chevron USA concerning its oil and gas exploration in the Malampaya region of the Philippines. For their prayers and counsel I'd like to acknowledge Renew Paris group members Susan Farrarons, Mary Anderson, Julia Jamison and Leila Tan Duclos.

For their prayers and counsel, I'll always owe a debt of gratitude to Prayer Warriors, Pastor Francis and Pastora Ching Nicolas with the Grain, New Wine and Oil Ministry.

Last but not least, thank you to my daughters Leslie and Christina, along with Christina's husband, Dan, for your encouragement, reminders, and salient observations as I pushed my book over the finish line.

I shall end with my favorite passage from the Good Book:

"Rejoice always. Pray without ceasing. In everything, give thanks."
1 Thessalonians 5:16

## OTHER BOOKS BY LOIDA NICOLAS LEWIS

**How the Filipino Veteran of WW2 Can Become a U.S. Citizen**
By Loida Nicolas Lewis

**How to Get a Green Card**
By Ilona Bray J.D. and Loida Nicolas Lewis

## OTHER BOOKS BY BLAIR S. WALKER

**Why Should White Guys Have All the Fun?: How Reginald Lewis Created a Billion-Dollar Business Empire**
By Reginald F. Lewis and Blair S. Walker

**Beating the Odds: Eddie Brown's Investing and Life Strategies**
By Eddie Brown and Blair S. Walker

**Inner City Miracle**
By Judge Greg Mathis and Blair S. Walker

**My Rise To The Stars: How A Sharecropper's Daughter Became An Army General**
By Clara Adams-Ender and Blair S. Walker

**I Can Do That!: Advice for Spiritual Entrepreneurs**
By Walter F. Johnson and Blair S. Walker

**Bill Clinton and Black America**
By Dewayne Wickham (Blair S. Walker, contributor)

**Up Jumped the Devil (A Darryl Billups Mystery, Book 1)**
By Blair S. Walker

**Hidden in Plain View (A Darryl Billups Mystery, Book 2)**
By Blair S. Walker

**Don't Believe Your Lying Eyes (A Darryl Billups Mystery, Book 3)**
By Blair S. Walker

## BOOKS ABOUT REGINALD F. LEWIS

**Reginald F. Lewis: Before TLC Beatrice**
By Lin Hart

**Lonely at the Top**
By Christina Lewis Halpern

**Keep Going No Matter What: Reginald F. Lewis: 20 Years Later**
By Loida Nicolas Lewis and Ponchitta Pierce

**REGINALD F LEWIS: A TRIBUTE**
**Remarks given in St. Edward Church, Baltimore, MD; Riverside Church, NYC; Harvard Law School, Cambridge, MA**
Edited by Elliott A. Wiley

# INDEX